Rooted in Scriptu[illegible] comprehensive, Jeremy [illegible] message needs to be considered and discussed by all pastors and church officers, as well as by all others who are concerned about where our future ministers will come from.

Stuart Olyott, author and retired pastor

I have two significant concerns as I look at the way men are pursuing a call into the ministry. My first concern is a lack of pastors investing time and resources to raise men up within their churches. My second concern is a lack of churches seeing their biblical responsibility to raise men up for ministry service. This is why the book you hold in your hands is so timely and important. This one book, *Passing the Baton*, addresses both of these critical areas and gives insightful and practical counsel on how pastors and churches can effectively raise up and equip the next generation of pastors, evangelists, and missionaries. Jeremy Walker has been faithfully mentored by older men as well as diligent to mentor others himself. He is a qualified and needed voice on what has become a lost focus in the modern church. Walker's advice is sound, wise, and biblical. I commend both the author and this book.

Brian Croft, founder and Executive Director, Practical Shepherding

I am delighted to commend enthusiastically this fine and timely little work on pastoral ministry. Jeremy Walker understands pastoral ministry 'from the inside' and his counsels are practical, thoughtful, mined from wide reading, and above all, biblical. The following quote immediately persuaded me that this was both a book to read and commend: "The best seminary training involves proven pastors and preachers (not simply scholars and theoreticians) passing on a theology that has been tested and depended on in the cut and thrust of church life, which has been proven in the crucible of ministerial labour." I would like every seminary student and every would-be gospel minister to read and digest this vade mecum (a book to carry with you).

Ian Hamilton, Editor, Banner of Truth

I wholeheartedly commend this little work for two reasons. First, the method proposed is thoroughly scriptural, therefore worthy of adoption if one desires the blessing of God in training men for the glory of God. Second, I know from my own experience that the author is a man who has sincerely sought to practice what he preaches in this little book. The principles laid out in this book are not the speculations of an academic, but realities that Jeremy has tried to implement in his own life and ministry. I am fortunate to be one among many who have been the beneficiary of this approach, and will seek to practice it myself.

Tom Allen, pastor, Eastbourne Grace Baptist Church

Passing the Baton

Passing the Baton

Jeremy Walker

EP BOOKS

(Evangelical Press) Unit C, Tomlinson Road, Leyland, PR25 2DY, England

epbooks.org
e-mail: sales@epbooks.org

First published in Great Britain in 2023

British Library Cataloguing in Publication Data

A record for this book is available from the British Library

ISBN 978–1–78397–351–4

Designed by Jordan Cox

Printed in the UK

This book is dedicated,
with deep gratitude,
to the men who graciously and patiently invested in me,
and, with deep commiseration,
to the gracious and patient men in whom I have tried to invest.

Contents

Introduction: the horror stories

You may have heard some of the stories. You may even have been in some of the stories.

There is the young man from Europe who was contemplating his future service in the church. He had a vague thought that some generic 'Bible' degree somewhere in America was the best way to set himself up for such a life. Or you have the seminary student with a theological degree but with no practical experience, sincerely and incompetently laying waste to the flock entrusted to his care. Or there stands the arrogant theological graduate, persuaded that his degree is the only qualification he needs for the work of ministry.

Perhaps it is the preacher flailing vigorously in the pulpit, thrashing about theologically, but showing no systematic instruction or awareness of the whole counsel of God. Or perhaps it is the gifted speaker who can carry the crowd but has little to say.

Maybe it is the earnest fellow desiring to be properly equipped for the work of the ministry. He has a working assumption that the only course open to him is a formal degree, and is mindlessly counselled by friends with a default setting of 'seminary' when it comes to training for service. Or it could be the equally earnest brother with an ingrained suspicion of anything formal when it comes to instruction. He is terrified of what he considers the inherently deadening effects of any sort of deliberate training, confident that it is the surest way to quench the Holy Spirit.

Have you heard the litany of complaints about the young preachers who have been coming to the church from the respected seminary? They are men with the best of intentions, no doubt, but clearly not preachers by constitution or instruction. Or it may be the testimonies of dismay, despair and even disgust about the rising generation of ministers. They give the impression of being men without a well-tempered bone in their backs and a well-governed tongue in their heads, slouching into pulpits, ill-equipped for the work that they have come to do.

You may know about the church that has endured a long and crippling 'interregnum' (a fearful word—the space between the kings!). That church has declined to a state of fussy passivity, inertly wondering where the next man will come from. You may be aware of the desperate congregation that appointed a preacher after one Sunday on which he delivered his two most sparkling sermons. (To be honest, they may have been the only two sermons he has ever preached that had any sparkle!) Now that church finds itself locked in an ugly ecclesiastical marriage with a man they do not know and who has no real regard for them.

There is the church that decides that something is better than nothing, and decides to compromise on some weighty issue in calling a man. It moves forward hoping that the fallout will not be too devastating.

And here is the man who hawks himself as a preacher or pastor for hire, and here the church which effectively swipes left and right, bestowing favour or disdain as they flick through the preening candidates. Together they act as if ministerial appointment were more like a dating application than a matter of spiritual life and health.

There is also the story about the church that did not quite know how to handle the obnoxious fellow who was persuaded he was called to preach, so they sent him off to seminary in the hopes that someone else would deal with the problem.

Perhaps you could add colour to these stories, or you could offer more stories. Perhaps you are one of the stories, or could tell worse stories. Perhaps you are inclined simply to shrug and to sit on your hands until Jesus comes back and makes it all better, or at least until the next revival.

Perhaps you hope that there is something better. You are right! Storytelling and shrugging are no proper responses to this situation. A righteous response requires biblical deliberation, deep-rooted conviction and principled action. We must begin with the sufficiency of Scripture and the centrality of the church.

1
Following the Bible

The apostle Paul was persuaded, and expected Timothy to be persuaded, that Scripture was first of all able to make someone 'wise for salvation through faith which is in Christ Jesus' (2 Tim. 3:15). He further impressed upon Timothy that 'all Scripture is given by inspiration of God, and is profitable for doctrine, for reproof, for correction, for instruction in righteousness, that the man of God may be complete, thoroughly equipped for every good work' (2 Tim. 3:16–17). The Word of God is all we need to address all the questions of righteousness, in principle and in practice, and rightly followed will cause us to live godly lives in Christ Jesus.

Paul also said to Timothy that he wrote some things 'so that you may know how you ought to conduct yourself in the house of God, which is the church of the living God, the pillar and ground of the truth' (1 Tim. 3:15). The church of God is the house of God, the place where God is in charge. It is the place which God orders for his glory, and therefore for the joy and blessing of all those who are brought under his roof.

It is no accident that these—and other such counsels—are found in what are often called the pastoral epistles. Here Paul expresses his convictions about the sufficiency of Scripture and the centrality of the church; in this context we find Paul's divinely inspired prescription for the challenge of equipping the next generation to serve the Lord.

Timothy was called upon to get, to guard and to give the truth in an environment marked by desertions and defections. Paul said to him, 'that good thing which was committed to you, keep by the Holy Spirit who dwells in us. This you know, that all those in Asia have turned away from me, among whom are Phygellus and Hermogenes' (2 Tim. 1:14–15). What a dreadful state of things! While all others are turning away, including what may have been the unusually shocking and distressing cases of Phygellus and Hermogenes, Timothy is to hold fast. Furthermore, he is to take deliberate action: 'the things that you have heard from me among many witnesses, commit these to faithful men who will be able to teach others also' (2 Tim. 2:2).

It is this specific command which we will be examining in the course of this book. Paul tells Timothy that he needs to take to heart the responsibility for equipping the next generation of pastors and preachers. He needs to entrust them with a deposit of truth for which they will be stewards in their turn. That responsibility, passed on through these pastoral epistles, continues to be the responsibility of the faithful pastors of faithful churches today. It is a particular duty for the shepherds of Christ's flock, but it is a duty in which every member of the flock has an interest. The duty to nurture, prepare, instruct and encourage a new generation of faithful men is one in which every thoughtful Christian and faithful congregation recognises their stake.

For pastors, it is a matter of passing the baton, ensuring that we do all we can to raise men who will walk in the footsteps of Christ in caring for his people. For churches, it is a question of who will shepherd our children, who will care for our souls in old age, who will equip the next generation of workers, who will hold the gospel torch high if the gloom deepens.

This matter of passing the baton is the closest thing you will find in the Bible to apostolic succession. Paul received the gospel he preached direct from heaven: 'I neither received it from man, nor was I taught it, but it came through the revelation of Jesus Christ' (Gal. 1:12). Paul was nurtured in some measure by Barnabas, but the teaching itself was of God. Paul then taught Timothy and others, committing to their charge the truth of the gospel. Now Paul calls Timothy to do the same in his turn, teaching other faithful men the things which he himself has received. These in their turn will pass on the same 'body of divinity' to others similarly qualified, and so on down the line.

This is the clear biblical model for ministerial training, for pastoral succession. Fundamentally, such training takes place under seasoned ministers in the context of the local church. I am therefore writing with those men in mind, and conscious that this is a responsibility in which they need to be encouraged and supported by local churches.

Show and tell

Paul delivers this charge to someone who is already the practically proven product of the very system he describes, working in the context of a local church. This was Paul's own model.

Timothy himself is the graduate of this select, though not quite exclusive, course. Paul could say of him, 'you have carefully followed my doctrine, manner of life, purpose, faith, longsuffering, love, perseverance, persecutions, afflictions, which happened to me at Antioch, at Iconium, at Lystra—what persecutions I endured. And out of them all the Lord delivered me' (2 Tim. 3:10–11). Timothy learned from Paul through the outward highs and lows of his apostolic career. What Paul said to the Corinthians as a whole, he could say to Timothy in particular: 'Imitate me, just as I also imitate Christ' (1 Cor. 11:1).

This is, to use more modern phrases, true discipling and real mentoring. It is teaching by example—a show-and-tell method of instruction which involves taking the learner under the wing of the teacher. Timothy had not only heard about this life, he had actually seen it. In this way he had learned the art of preaching, and the reality of pressure, and the power of prayer, and the nature of pains, and the challenges of persecution. Now he is called to guard that same gospel which Paul has been faithful to guard. He is to guard it by way of personal strength, for which he must look to Christ. He is to guard it by way of passing it on, for which he must invest in Christ's men. Timothy is to adopt this model of in-house, hands-on equipping for ministry.

The place of seminary

Historically, I think one might see the best of the mentoring system in the days before and around the Log College. This was an independent institution for learning, founded in 1727 by Gilbert Tennent in what is now Warminster in Pennsylvania, USA. Up to that time, formal ministerial training was typically carried out at Yale and Harvard. However, these were days in which those aspiring to the work of the ministry—with and without more formal academic instruction—typically went to live with an older pastor. They served under the more experienced man, watching and listening, always learning, sharpening their sense of the work and developing their capacity for it.

The best seminary training involves proven pastors and preachers (not simply scholars and theoreticians) passing on a theology that has been tested and depended on in the cut and thrust of church life, which has been proven in the crucible of ministerial labour. Where ministerial training becomes the exclusive province of professionals, it will inevitably become divorced from the realities of practical pastoring. When men who do not or cannot preach are teaching others to preach, they will rarely help a true preaching gift.

The system which Paul advocates puts the church and her pastors back where they belong, at the very heart of God's purposes for the sustaining of his kingdom. I am chilled by the oft-repeated mantra, 'As goes the seminary, so goes the church.' If that is true, then it may actually indicate that the church has already surrendered its proper calling and function in this regard. It might reveal that pastors have already relinquished their responsibility to pass the baton. We might legitimately lament how often and how foolishly the church, under her elders, has surrendered its centrality and primacy as the institution established by Christ for the preservation and proclamation of the gospel of the kingdom.

Alternatively, that phrase might suggest that the seminary, deliberately or otherwise, has supplanted the church. Seminaries might co-opt to themselves a centrality and primacy that they were never intended to have. If there is to be any specialised sphere for pastoral instruction, it is those already serving the church who should be directing and influencing it. No church and no eldership should simply relinquish its responsibilities towards the men it sends into more formal theological training.

Seminary may be the best option, or a good option, for a particular man, but I would still insist, based on Paul's words, that Paul's model of mentoring is both the best preparative for seminary and the best finishing school afterwards. The particular care of serving pastors in a local church may, in fact, be a preferable alternative to the seminary. Today, distance learning can provide an opportunity to enjoy the sunshine of more academic instruction while remaining rooted in the soil of the local church.

Where seminary training is not the best option, or an option at all, it is a rare man who does not need some kind of model and instruction as to how he goes about the work. It is remarkable how some of the finest pastor-teachers have benefited from this pastoral passing the baton, more deliberately or incidentally.

An atmosphere of nurture

There is a question as to whether or not, especially as ministers of the gospel, we are humble enough to pursue this course. In too many churches there is a centralising, and even a hoarding, of what is perceived to be power. The pulpit is guarded not just from error, as it should be, but from any other voice or personality. Other gifts are perceived to be threats to the primacy or supremacy of 'the one'. In some congregations there is a carelessness, sometimes misrepresented as trust in God, concerning the future of the church and its faithful ministry. Men who show promise are thrust out, not so much into the harvest field as the wilderness, without being taught how to plough the ground, plant the seed and gather a crop. Would-be shepherds, with real gifts and manifest graces, are pushed into the margins of church life, where their gifts wither and their graces grow flabby.

It may seem as if there is only one person who can be the hero of every church-life narrative. A system which unhealthily reserves and restricts all usefulness in ministry to one, or an unrighteously favoured few, is contrary to the health of the church. This is as true for Baptists and Congregationalists as it is for Presbyterians, and remains true whether the restriction is deliberate or merely neglectful.

As we shall see, that is certainly not the same as saying that everyone could be or should be a preacher or teacher (compare James 3:1). It is not to deny that in most congregations there is one person who is particularly gifted for public ministry and who rightly has the lion's share of that privilege and duty. It is to say that pastors should actively seek to cultivate the gifts of others, even if they might come to overshadow their own. Indeed, if we have a right spirit, that prospect should give us great joy.

Are we, deliberately or otherwise, creating a culture of dependence on man or a spirit of shortsightedness in our congregations? Are elders—including vocational ministers—fostering an environment in which there is no expectation of, or investment in, future generations of useful servants of the Word? Are we even suspicious of the gifts of others?

Such a spirit is fatal to the whole atmosphere of the New Testament. The gifts and graces that the Lord grants to his church are to be identified, assessed, cultivated, celebrated and employed. Again, that is not to say that a church and her pastors should mindlessly embrace every ignorant or arrogant claim to preaching and teaching capacity. It does mean that it would be a folly and a sin in a church to deny or neglect the genuine gifts that the Head of the church is bestowing upon his beloved people, for his own glory and for their good.

There are many men and churches who have understood this. They have understood it without feeling the need to broadcast or boast about their labours. They do not parade their efforts or demand donations for their work (a work often unknown to all but themselves and their beneficiaries, and to God). They have simply taken the feeble shoots of would-be pastors and preachers into the greenhouse of their own ministry and nurtured them until they are ready to be planted.

Adopting the apostolic model

I want to make clear that I write as one who has

benefited from the kind of system that I describe. My primary qualification for writing is less that of one who has a thousand other men under my wing, and more that of a man who has profited from being under the wing of others. I can hear the voices and see the faces of several men who have taken time and pains to pour themselves into my life. Those men have instructed, corrected and exhorted me. Some have done so very deliberately and intimately. Others have done so at a slightly greater distance, perhaps less aware of their influence upon me, but it is the men who have got closest who have helped most. I have tried to imitate them as they have imitated Christ. I have watched and listened as other men have done this to their protégés, and seen the benefit when it has been done well. I believe that they have passed the baton to me, and I believe I have a responsibility to pass it to others in my turn.

I have seen something, sadly, of the damage when this has been done in a careless or shallow way. I have sat down with brothers who have come crying out for someone who will be, under God, a friend and a help to them along the way. Some have felt isolated and exposed, even betrayed or abandoned. As time has passed, it has been my privilege to try, in some small measure, to repay towards others the best investments I have enjoyed.

A young fellow stumbles through his early sermons. A phone call comes in about what to do with a certain pastoral conundrum. A self-conscious young man arrives at a conference for the first time. An email arrives asking for input into a particular situation or a whole life. An opportunity comes to preach to other pastors. As these doors open, as these new relationships develop, as these developed friendships deepen, I am simply passing on privileges already received.

If we, as church members, and as ministers of the gospel in particular, are ourselves persuaded of the sufficiency of Scripture, then we are obliged to adopt this apostolic and pastoral model. Pastors of churches must deliberately and proactively set out to fulfil the command of 2 Timothy 2:2: 'And the things that you have heard from me among many witnesses, commit these to faithful men who will be able to teach others also.'

Every pastor and every church must consider what this means and pursue what it requires. From my heart I would encourage the men who are given a charge to lead and serve the churches to embrace this opportunity, within and alongside the church as a whole. It is the responsibility of the whole congregation, and particularly of those who are shepherds among the flock.

Passing the baton in this way requires of us an investment. Passing the baton is an additional investment, in that it requires something above and beyond other aspects of the work. It is a selective investment, in that the elders must carefully identify those particular men who are equipped to receive it. It is a deliberate investment, in that it must be planned and purposeful. Passing the baton is a personal investment, a warm relationship in which not just real fellowship but genuine friendship often develops. It is a gracious investment, in that the pastor is trying to inform the character and develop the gifts of someone else, and not simply impose himself and his personality on another. It is a sacrificial investment, proving costly for the mentor and the one being mentored, as well as for the church in which this all takes place. It is an urgent investment, because time is short and we do not know how long any of us might have. It is a long-term investment, because—however soon we begin—the outcome may take years and bear fruit over decades. It is a shared investment, because pastors and churches should be engaging together in the work, assisting and encouraging one another. It is a beneficial investment, bringing encouragements and delights to those who participate in the work. Passing the baton is a Christlike investment, in that the pastor who makes it is not merely following in the footsteps of Paul, but imitating Christ himself.

It must be a prayerful investment, for without the smile of heaven upon the work there will be no progress. It is a responsibility which is pastoral, congregational and personal. We will consider these aspects of the work of passing the baton in the chapters which follow.

2
An additional investment

Every minister, following in the footsteps of the apostles, should have as his priorities prayer and the ministry of the Word of God (Acts 6:4). Pastors must gather, and guide, and guard, and govern the flock of Christ entrusted to their care. They give themselves to those under their care in Christlike fashion. This will obviously include preaching to unbelievers and ministering to the saints, as well as various other opportunities, duties and responsibilities.

We have now recognised that there is at least one further aspect of the work which must be considered, the labour which Paul encouraged in and required of Timothy: 'And the things that you have heard from me among many witnesses, commit these to faithful men who will be able to teach others also' (2 Tim. 2:2).

So there will need to be an additional investment. It is above and beyond the other aspects of pastoral ministry, while still very much a part of it. It is a dimension of church life that might easily be overlooked. It involves a work of discipling, by means of which (to use the apostle John's categories) the little children are trained up to become young men, and the young men mature into fathers.

Taking opportunities

The specific investment in faithful men will be a particular element of the work of ministering to the saints. It will almost certainly involve something over and above the regular course of ministry. It will be very easy for this to be swallowed up by the normal and pressing duties of sermon preparation, wider reading and other study, pastoral visiting, and so on. It may be one of those points at which the tyranny of the urgent threatens to swallow up the consideration of the important.

It is clear by the way in which Paul introduces this duty to Timothy that it is by no means an *optional* extra. Timothy is exhorted and commanded to commit what he has learned to others. In the light of this, it is disappointing how often passing the baton appears to be an overlooked element of the work. Perhaps it is not just a lack of time. It may be that there is some kind of fear, and with some good reason. It may be that a false humility or a real confusion prevents a solid and reliable man from getting on with this work. He may have become persuaded that this work belongs to ten-talent men, to the shooting stars of the evangelical heavens, to those who have substantial followings and larger material resources at their disposal.

It is also worth remembering that it is not inherently sinful or even a necessary failure not to have this opportunity. No man should beat himself up if, in the course of steady ministry over years or decades, the Lord does not give him these opportunities, despite prayer and preparation for them. However, if there is no prayer or preparation, then we cannot necessarily expect the Lord to provide us with those opportunities. The Lord Christ is sovereign in the dispensation of his gifts. Even much prayer might bring about the answer, 'no' or, 'not yet'. At the same time, some of these opportunities might not present themselves in an obvious way. Perhaps even a few words in a sermon somewhere, or a brief conversation in the margins of some seemingly insignificant meeting, might prove a real blessing to some brother who goes on to minister the Word of God. He might do so far more fruitfully than the unknown man who was his encourager and helper. The great Puritan John Owen found peace of heart through the preaching of an unknown preacher when the expected 'big name' was not able to preach at the appointed time and place. Who knows what a blessing you might be to someone, without ever knowing?

A wide view

The people in whom we invest may not necessarily be members of the church which we serve. We are certainly not to be parochial. We may have openings around us and along the way that will benefit others rather than ourselves.

It may not always be a systematic investment. Suppose you are asked to preach at a special meeting for a church, or to participate in a small conference. What if you were asked questions by a young man in whose heart your preaching has struck a chord? Could you not offer some counsels and encouragements? You could invite him to keep in touch, letting his pastor know that you have done so. Why not, in concert with other local churches, create an environment in which you could variously host the budding preachers and give them counsel? You might sit down next to a weary younger brother at a pastors' gathering, or find that the local fraternal has two or three fellow-servants who feel out of their depth. There may be any number of opportunities which, over time, could accumulate into a real deposit of blessing in a number of different lives and different churches.

Of course, this investment has to be made in accordance with our graces, gifts and opportunities. We are not called to do what we cannot or should not do, but we are called to do this specific work as we are able. It is an investment which the whole church needs to recognise, so that it can be made by the elders without resentment or resistance.

One great danger in passing the baton is the threat, real or perceived, of sheep-stealing. We must be wary of offending a brother, so contacts with members of other churches need to be personally and graciously communicated to the minister or elders of that church.

Sadly, there are too many examples of poor behaviour in this area to ignore. For example, one pastor told me of an approach made to his own son by another man. This man was inviting the son out of the church in which he was a member, suggesting that he might be able to find a use for him. Whatever the motive, the failure to consult the young man's pastor and father was both personally rude and a poor example of church relations.

In a second case, a seminary student recounted the tale of a minister invited to the seminary to introduce his denomination to a class of students. The minister waited until seminary staff were absent, then suggested to the students that his denomination had plenty on offer for such men as they were. He could easily open a way into any number of good posts with attractive salaries and properties, with plenty of perks and opportunities for advancement. Any suggestion of such a carnal approach is the opposite of what the apostle Paul intends in the instructions we are considering.

Whether we have wider opportunities or not, Paul's injunction that Timothy should 'commit these [things which he has received] to faithful men who will be able to teach others also' (2 Tim. 2:2) assumes something additional to the regular public ministry to the whole church. The regular preaching and teaching of the Word certainly lays the foundation for this. Still, a more definite and deliberate investment is required in order to pass the baton. It is at once more intensive and more expansive, requiring particular instruction to particular individuals, or a small group of individuals.

3
A selective investment

Timothy himself was distinctive in his own native context: 'He was well spoken of by the brethren who were at Lystra and Iconium' (Acts 16:2). He is to make the same kind of assessments in his current sphere (probably, in this case, Ephesus). He is to identify men with both the grace to learn and the gift to teach, men to whom he can pass the pastoral baton. This requires a selective investment, in which a pastor guides a church to identify the particular men who can receive this particular teaching. Both the grace to learn and the gift to teach are vital.

The grace to learn

With regard to this first prerequisite, I will paraphrase

John Owen's experience of life as an educator: many men are doctors in their first year, masters by their second, and only begin to become learners by their third. Think of the young man, a seminarian, who visited a church to preach. After the sermon, the pastor—a man of some thirty years' experience in the ministry—asked the young man if he might appreciate some feedback on the sermon. 'What for?' inquired the arrogant novice. It was quite evident that he could not comprehend that he should need any particular improvement. What should we do with such a man? I suggest we could pray that the Lord might humble him before he does damage either to his own soul or the souls of others! Or what of the fellow who, recently graduated and installed alongside an older man, mentioned with a wink that they were both well aware of his competence. He made clear that his responsibilities in that place were simply a marking of the time until others became aware of his gifts and snapped him up. God spare the church who cannot see further than the external sparkle of such a performer!

On the other hand, perhaps you have had the joy of dealing with a thirsty drinker, of investing in an eager listener and learner. He does not resent instruction. He positively yearns for feedback and acts upon it. He hears and heeds the suggestions and instructions that are offered. He may not always enjoy the process, and he may not be afraid to push back, but he is determined to profit by it. He is no mindless novice but an intelligent student, processing what he is told and properly assimilating it. These are, primarily, the men into whom we should pour our time and effort. Give me every time a man of meagre gift, with grace to learn, over the dazzling gift without the open ear and humble heart!

As these men are still learning, they are almost certainly part-proved rather than fully proven. The question at this point is probably not whether or not you will appoint them to eldership. They should be manifestly healthy members of a genuinely healthy congregation, interacting with others. They must have begun to show the evidences of men who can take and hold the truth. They are not, and need not yet be, the finished article; nevertheless, there is a growing aptitude and appetite for learning, and a developing aptitude and appetite for teaching. Timothy is to look for men who are more or less what he was when he was at their spiritual age and stage of life.

The primary qualification at this stage is budding faithfulness. These brothers may not always have much truth to which they cling, but they show a readiness to cling tenaciously to the truth they know. It is the same quality that is required of elders (and deacons) in their spheres. There is an obvious and proper overlap, because these are the kind of men who will serve in office once the baton has been passed.

Trustworthiness

What we have here is fundamentally the language of trustworthiness. It speaks of being proved in an environment in which fraudulent paths open up, and many are drifting into dangerous or even fatal byways. Timothy himself is exhorted to 'guard what was committed to your trust, avoiding the profane and idle babblings and contradictions of what is falsely called knowledge' (1 Tim. 6:20) and to 'shun profane and idle babblings, for they will increase to more ungodliness' (2 Tim. 2:16).

There are many men who—'as Jannes and Jambres resisted Moses'—'resist the truth: men of corrupt minds, disapproved concerning the faith' (2 Tim. 3:8). It is a time when 'evil men and impostors will grow worse and worse, deceiving and being deceived' (2 Tim. 3:13). Yes, there are perilous seasons at hand. 'For the time will come when they will not endure sound doctrine, but according to their own desires, because they have itching ears, they will heap up for themselves teachers; and they will turn their ears away from the truth, and be turned aside to fables'

(2 Tim. 4:3–4). Hardly a walk in the park! And it is in this wilderness world that Timothy is to find trustworthy men in whom he can make this multi-faceted investment.

Such men are among the saints, already demonstrating the capacity to hold fast to the truth, and then to hand it on to others in their turn. These are men who listen to, learn and love the truth. They are willing and able to communicate it to others. They are not dreamers and innovators, but rather declarers and imitators. We do not want men with an appetite for novelty, but a reputation for integrity.

But how do we discern such men? The church of Jesus Christ is the primary environment in which such graces and gifts come to light. We should be hoping for members to be nudging the elders and asking, 'Have you thought about young Master Green?' or, 'What about giving old Mr Grey a little more scope?' The whole church should be looking out for men who can, by God's grace, bear this load. Our pastoral antennae must be alert to the emergence of such men in the congregation. We must be prayerfully and proactively looking out for such gifts of Christ.

Developing gifts

Passing the baton requires such an investment, even a

holy risk at times. We must, of course, guard the pulpit against error and incompetence. At the same time, we should not build the walls so high that it is impossible to get into it, nor shape the door so that only one man fits through it. Some go so far as to say that if, after a number of years, a particular man is still the only one in the church who can or does teach or preach, that man is already failing. If no-one else is showing or using any ability to teach, how good a teacher have you actually proved to be? Some men have particular scope. In a seminary town, a church might have a fairly steady stream of men with some appetite for ministry. In other places, it may be one or two in a generation who show the will and the ability for the work. A big city might provide a fairly constant stream of possibilities but with a high turnover rate. A small village might give opportunity for a long-term investment in a few good men.

The elders of a church might need to find or create avenues in which a teaching and preaching capacity can be publicly tested and developed. This might be in the Sunday school classes, an adult Bible class, street evangelism, home Bible studies, leading the public worship, and so on. We shall require wisdom to give the appropriate opportunities, to assess and to invest.

We must remember, too, that there are any

number of men who felt their own inadequacy (real or imagined) so keenly that they struggle even to get into a pulpit a second time. Some failed miserably in their early attempts. Others were slow in developing, needing much nurture even to get over the first hurdles. Might we have crushed or dismissed a John Newton, an Andrew Fuller, or a William Carey? There may need to be wise encouragement and careful direction of some men whose gifts need to be developed over time, and the rough edges gradually smoothed.

Some may take ten or fifteen attempts before there is a settled demonstration of the presence (or, indeed, the absence) of the appropriate capacities. Some will receive investment that may not lead, ultimately, to holding office in the church. However, it may still equip them, in measure, to be better private students of the Scripture, better husbands and fathers, better leaders of family devotion, better teachers in Sunday schools, and so on.

Wisdom and courage

Pastors will therefore need the courage to say, 'Yes!' to some men, 'Maybe!' to others, 'Later!' to a few, 'Soon!' to some, and a plain 'No!' to several. We will need the patience and fortitude to say, 'Try again!' to those who are fearful, and, 'Not yet!' to those who are running ahead of themselves. There are some men who are persuaded—in the absence of any healthy ecclesiastical sanction—that the Lord has his hand upon them. I know of at least one man who went to seminary because his church was afraid to tell him he should not and could not pursue the ministry. That church therefore signed off the papers that took him off their hands. That is a shocking dereliction of duty on the part of the church and her elders. The ensuing misery cannot be entirely blamed on the seminary, although one might hope that such men might be graciously weeded out before they do much harm to God's people. Other brothers need much nurture, and even then may reach a certain point and level out. They will need to be told, 'Thus far but no further, at least at this point in time.'

Some men become competent occasional preachers, but their developing character, particular graces, exegetical skills, emotional range, vocal capacity, intellectual (not necessarily academic) potential, willingness and ability to work hard, and so on will keep them from advancing unless there is some further development in them. Some men need to be prodded, urged and encouraged to do a little more. They can be reticent to the point of being cowardly, and need to be exhorted to step up and press on, and to give what they have to offer. Others think they can run when they can barely walk, or are just learning to trot. They may need firm words about what is needed to equip them for the work that they may one day be able to undertake.

Under the oversight of the elders, the church needs the convictions and the courage to invest in particular men, the ones who have shown some ability to learn and to teach, and who need the opportunity to grow.

4
A deliberate investment

The investment required to pass the baton in this way will never 'just happen'. You cannot incidentally or accidentally commit a lifetime's learning 'to faithful men who will be able to teach others also' (2 Tim. 2:2). It cannot be occasional, careless or random. Many plants will not truly flourish if they are only checked and pruned at odd seasons every few years. In the same way, these processes of investment in men will not produce much fruit if you only think of them from time to time. This cannot be a task that the elders carry out 'off the cuff'. Rather, it will need to be more thoughtful, planned and systematic.

The deposit of truth

Paul told Timothy to 'hold fast the pattern of sound words which you have heard from me, in faith and love which are in Christ Jesus' (2 Tim. 1:13). He had passed on to his student a publicly attested pattern of truth. The defined and dogmatic deposit of divine truth that Timothy received from Paul is the same deposit of truth that he must in turn pass on to others.

To be sure, Timothy would have had many occasional and incidental moments of learning. There is much in the relationship that might be like that of a father with a child: 'You shall teach them diligently to your children, and shall talk of them when you sit in your house, when you walk by the way, when you lie down, and when you rise up' (Deut. 6:7). There will be moments on a journey, over a meal and along the way in which truth can be imparted and reinforced. Nevertheless, Paul had taken pains to ensure that Timothy knew a system of truth that was clear and consistent. No doubt there were sessions of more intense instruction, opportunities for broad and deep teaching, that developed along the road. No doubt Timothy listened carefully to the sermons that Paul preached. No doubt Paul took up and expanded the substance and the themes of those sermons. Luke would have been travelling with them at times, as well as other preachers and teachers, and their insights would perhaps have been an additional help.

I do not doubt that passing the baton would have included direction towards a proper understanding of the whole of the Scriptures as then possessed. It would have involved the centrality of the messianic hope in the covenant of grace. It would have demonstrated the incremental nature of God's revelation with the unfolding of the covenants of promise, the increasing visibility and clarity of God's saving truth. There would have been instruction and example as to how the Word of God should be handled. Paul would have communicated a way of understanding and interpreting the Bible in keeping with that of the other apostles, under the illuminating influence of the Holy Spirit.

Passing the baton might have included a very clear and specific testimony of the truth of Christ's life, death and resurrection, filling in any details that Timothy did not already know. There might not have been much in the way of 'church history' to study, in the modern sense. Nevertheless, Timothy may well have been told not just about the recorded experience of the Old Testament people of God, but the immediate experience of the saints of the new covenant community since it was formally inaugurated. We cannot imagine that the man who wrote the letter to the church at Rome would fail to give Timothy a systematic understanding of the truth: it is of the very essence of the phrase, 'the pattern of sound words'.

No doubt, too, Paul would have explained the qualities of character and the elements of calling that he expected from Timothy. In Paul, Timothy would have seen a man fiercely committed to the truth and at once forthright and gentle in his dealings with others. He would have seen a man contending without compromise when the truth was under threat, and communicating with patience when there was ignorance or confusion. The proper care of the flock of Christ—its provision and protection—would have been a central element. Timothy would also have learned the significant elements of a godly life: the integrity of a man of God, his reliability, his orderliness, his diligence, his kindness, his generosity, his timeliness, his patience, his contentment, his prayerfulness.

By the end of this course, the baton had been passed. Paul could say to Timothy that 'you have carefully followed my doctrine, manner of life, purpose, faith, longsuffering, love, perseverance, persecutions, afflictions' (2 Tim. 3:10–11). All the departments of religious truth would have been adequately addressed, driven element by element into Timothy's eager soul. All the aspects of godly life would have been described or displayed for emulation. The result would have been a defined and dogmatic deposit of divine truth, known and felt. Paul would not have been concerned to give Timothy a list of options—he is not offering some of the possible opinions that men might hold on certain issues. He would have had no appetite for the inherent vagueness of the postmodern mind. He cared nothing for the wild inconsistencies of religious pluralism, for the bewildering landscape of ecclesiastical confusion, or for the uncharted wastes of moral relativism. He had no instinct toward a misguided sense of charity that only emphasises a number of more-or-less-right possible answers.

Men of conviction

This is true pastoral investment. Paul deliberately and systematically imparted a dogmatic deposit of divine truth to his young friend. Timothy was to pass on that deposit to others, telling them what was true and what was false. Neither Timothy nor those who would follow him were sitting in ivory towers, pondering vague possibilities and theorising about theologies. They were being sent out as sheep among wolves to gather, guide and guard God's flock. Such men need to know not the dreams of mere academics but the tools of true practitioners.

In the same way, we must, under God, breed men of conviction. There is little value in a man who can simply parrot back to you all the things that you believe without appropriating them for himself. There is little profit in a man who finishes a course of theological instruction with the understanding that most things do not matter very much. I am occasionally frustrated by the apparent desire of some instructors and institutions to dilute the deposit and blur the boundaries of truth, encouraging what they perceive as open-mindedness. They are passing on a baguette rather than a baton! Their students receive, in practice, not much more than ill-defined and ill-founded vagueness. The products of such a system are almost wilfully non-committal.

Some will have to go further. There will be some particular theological dangers that need to be identified. Certain times and places might require that younger men be instructed in the dangers of certain thinkers, worldviews or theological approaches (especially those which are presently fashionable). Men exposed to certain teachers or seminary courses may need a dose of 'counter-dogmatics' to get them back on the theological straight and narrow. That might be anything from the question of Barthian thought, creeping antinomianism, developing liberalism or lurking legalism, to trendy notions of the church, or irreverent and carnal approaches to the worship of God. The more plausible, persuasive or popular the error, the more careful and thorough one might need to be to expose and correct it.

Road-tested truth

One of the benefits of this better approach is that this is road-tested truth. This is instruction by men who have contended for truth. They are passing on the baton that they themselves have carried in the race. They have preached this truth from the pulpit, they have counselled and comforted troubled Christians, and they have instructed and directed confused Christians. The teachers have put their money where their mouth is.

The aim of such teachers must be an intelligent persuasion of apostolic truth and tradition that leads to real conviction and principled action. This is passing the baton. The church needs men who know that there is truth, and who know the truth. They must grasp truth as real and enduring. They must be able to receive it, and guard it themselves in their believing and living, and then pass on a definitive and dogmatic deposit to other men in their turn.

5
A personal investment

The people we are talking about are real people. These are the flesh-and-blood men who have been taken under our wing in order that we might pass on the deposit of truth in accordance with 2 Timothy 2:2. This is real mentoring, a particular element of discipling. It is true teaching. Each such person to whom we pass the baton needs a measure of personal attention.

Some men need someone to prompt them, to urge them on and draw them out. Some need someone who will channel and direct their energies into helpful courses. Some may need someone who will rein them in a little, before they gallop off and do themselves and others an injury. Some need someone to tell them what they have still to learn.

Perhaps you long for such a relationship? You believe that the Lord may be calling you to the ministry of the Word, but you are not sure what comes next. You may wish that there were someone who would invest in you and mould you, help you and direct you, who would keep you from trouble if possible and help you in trouble when it inevitably comes.

The help you needed

Perhaps, on the other hand, there was such a man and such a relationship for you—a man who took you under his wing? From whom did you learn? What does it mean to you to learn truth? Who taught you to pray, perhaps simply by example, so that you began to grasp what real prayer was? Who sat down with you after your first stumbling attempts at public ministry and explained everything, from the proper pronunciation of words to the proper interpretation and application of those words? Who took the time to walk you through your sermons before you preached them? Who did you call that week when you got into a panic on a Saturday afternoon because you had hit a host of roadblocks in your preparation for the Sunday sermons? Who talked you off the ledge on Monday morning after your sermon fell to pieces (perhaps in the very act of preaching) on the Lord's day, and you were on the verge of quitting preaching forever? Who picked you up and mended the cracks when someone took you apart without mercy for some flaw or failing, real or imagined?

The help you offer

Now look the other way. To whom are you that man? How many lives have you touched in this way? Early in his ministry, our Lord 'appointed twelve, that they might be with Him and that He might send them out to preach' (Mark 3:14). That 'with him' relationship is vital, and is seen all the way through the Scriptures.

You see it in Moses in his labours, when Joshua was with him. When Elijah knew that his ministry would come to an end, who was with him, if not Elisha? When Christ walked through Judea, the disciples were with him. When Paul was first converted, he was with Barnabas. When Paul went out on his journeys, Timothy and many others were with him—men like Titus and Silas and John Mark and Tychicus and Luke and Epaphras. They went out from him and returned to him. He continued to counsel and comfort them. You might add in Aquila and Priscilla, and they then did something similar with Apollos (Acts 18:24–26). Though he was already a gifted man, they nevertheless took Apollos aside and explained to him the way of God more accurately.

You can see how the ripples of instruction radiate

outward. One friend who enjoyed something of these kinds of relationship was an advocate of the following chain of discipleship: 'I do. You watch. We talk.' > 'I do. You help. We talk.' > 'You do. I help. We talk.' > 'You do. I watch. We talk.' > 'You do. Someone else watches. You talk.' The instruction here is more than public teaching and preaching. It involves personal and private investment. Those involved learn to do the same to and for others.

An apostolic example

This was what Paul invested in Timothy, when he was passing the baton. When Paul 'came to Derbe and Lystra,' Luke tells us, 'a certain disciple was there, named Timothy, the son of a certain Jewish woman who believed, but his father was Greek.' This young man 'was well spoken of by the brethren who were at Lystra and Iconium' (Acts 16:1–2). Paul took that young man under his wing, and Timothy began to be 'with him'. It is why he could say to Timothy, in time, 'you have carefully followed my doctrine, manner of life, purpose, faith, longsuffering, love, perseverance, persecutions, afflictions, which happened to me at Antioch, at Iconium, at Lystra—what persecutions I endured' (2 Tim. 3:10–11). Timothy had been personally instructed and tutored in the seminary of Paul. He had learned what it was, at first hand, to imitate Paul just as Paul imitated Christ (1 Cor. 11:1).

This does not mean, as we shall see, that there is no scope for proper delegation in this matter. It does not prohibit all formal and academic instruction. Those are separate questions, but I do suggest that a personal, close, active, warm, natural relationship between men of God in the context of a local church is at the root of passing the baton.

It is true not just of the beginnings of labour, but all along the way. Towards the end of his life, Paul is still writing to the man whom he calls his 'true son in the faith', his 'beloved son' (1 Tim. 1:2; 2 Tim. 1:2). Timothy's development has changed the dynamic but has not killed this relationship. Paul still thinks of him with fondness when he talks about the men he can really rely on. He can say of Timothy to the Philippians, 'you know his proven character, that as a son with his father he served with me in the gospel' (Phil. 2:22). It would have been the natural relational channel of instruction and investment, care and oversight. It was developed with depth and warmth in the spiritual relationship of Paul and Timothy. That is real discipleship.

I hear men who have come through different environments, including some seminaries, who speak of having a mentor for their years of training.

'Well,' I asked, 'what did you do?'

'Every six months or so we had a fireside chat,' was one answer I got.

'What did that involve?'

'Oh,' came the reply, 'I would go and sit down in his house and he would give me a cup of tea. We had had no real significant conversation for weeks. He would ask, "How is it going?" "Alright," I said. "Good," he replied. "Did you see the football the other night?"'

Real friendship

Men need to learn how to talk to each other! Even some pastors, whose gift of speech is their bread and butter, need to learn to relate by means of words, and to go on learning to do so. That can be hard for men for whom pouring out their hearts in public and private ministry is exhausting, leaving them wanting a little space and peace. It can be hard for men who have an expansive and engaging personality, but who might still struggle to let others close to them. Typically, men do not and will not communicate in the same way that women do, nor should that be expected of them. But I am not suggesting that men only grunt! In the Garden of Eden, it was Adam who was given the responsibility of using words to frame the world that God had made. Men ought to be noble talkers. With that in mind, there is an affection and an openness that needs to be fostered in real, masculine friendship, forged in labour together.

Harry Billinge was a soldier who stormed the Normandy beaches during D-Day in World War Two. Interviewed on the seventy-fifth anniversary of D-Day, he said this:

> All I know is, Normandy veterans love one another beyond the love of women. If you was in a hole in the ground with a bloke, you got to know him! Marvellous men!

I do not know from which part of his memory or experience Harry dredged up that phrase about love, but he is drawing on David's mournful celebration of his friend, Jonathan: 'Your love to me was wonderful, surpassing the love of women' (2 Sam. 1:26). There is something about being in a ministerial hole with another man, in the battle-scarred ground of church ministry, that develops real and lasting affection. That kind of depth does not come from an occasional cup of tea. Threat and danger, hardship and labour, are what forge deep bonds between brothers-in-arms. If you develop this relationship with another, then that well-laid foundation often provides for a sturdy superstructure that can be added to over time.

It is the kind of relationship that is beautifully demonstrated by two Johns, Newton and

Ryland. This is wonderfully set out in a book of their correspondence called *Wise Counsel: John Newton's Letters to John Ryland Jr.*[1] Ryland, who was precociously gifted, came early under Newton's gracious, thoughtful and valuable influence. That influence continued to bless and inform Ryland until his older friend's death. Reading the book provides us with a model of the kind of investment that bears much fruit.

Parenting and pastoring

In some circumstances, one challenge is that young men (and women) may need and want to be parented, perhaps before they can be pastored. I wonder if this lies behind so much of the demand that some young men have for someone just to spend time with them? It is not wrong to spend an hour or so in a coffee shop once a week with someone. It is, however, striking how much of that can simply be the appreciation of someone to talk to, someone by whom you can be loved and from whom you can receive a lasting gift of affection. Some of those who seek what they think is mentoring really just need to settle into regular church life, sit under the ministry of God's Word, and enjoy the affection and attention of all the saints in their proper roles and relationships. Pastors would be wise to take that into

1 Grant Gordon (ed.), *Wise Counsel: John Newton's Letters to John Ryland Jr.* (Edinburgh: Banner of Truth, 2009).

account when pressured by someone who demands to be Discipled or Mentored (you can usually hear the capitals). All of us would be wise to consider what we really want and need when seeking out those who will invest in us.

At the same time, it is no accident that Paul speaks to Timothy and to Titus as his sons in the faith (1 Tim. 1:2 and Tit. 1:4). At its best, and in a proper way, this relationship goes beyond the merely personal and pastoral to the genuinely paternal.

6
A gracious investment

There is a danger in a relationship such as that which I am describing. On the one hand, it is perfectly proper for the disciple to be like the master in some respects. I recall Ted Donnelly, a pastor and scholar in the Reformed Presbyterian Church of Northern Ireland, talking about the relationship between Professor John Murray, the Presbyterian scholar and preacher, and Albert Martin, a Reformed Baptist pastor-preacher. According to Pastor Donnelly, Al Martin was preaching at a conference, describing from the pulpit the proper effect on a preacher of highly esteemed older men. As he did this, he was emulating some of the pulpit mannerisms of Professor Murray, much to the delight of the older man who was then sitting in the congregation.

There was an almost-deliberate, near-instinctive embrace of some of Murray's distinctive gestures that arose out of affection and esteem.

Such stories and examples are sweet. However, many pastors have strong personalities. I do not necessarily mean aggressive or abrasive, but certainly often distinctive and pungent. Such men develop strong personal convictions over the course of their ministries. They can accumulate idiosyncrasies of style and substance, often in abundance. These can become dangerous if they are not well-handled, by the man himself and by others impressed by him.

Copycats

Sometimes an impressionable younger (or older) man deliberately apes their pulpit hero. Hopefully, they will grow out of such childishness. Sometimes, it is done entirely unawares, like the Yorkshire acolyte of Dr Martyn Lloyd-Jones who unwaveringly prayed in a Welsh accent. Perhaps you have seen the man who wears the same suit in the same colour as the Great Leader? He wears the same tie, and ties the same knot in it. He uses the same pen. He wears the same glasses. He removes them at the same point in his sentences to make the same emphasis in the same way. He might remove his suit jacket at precisely the same point in the service, or he leans on the pulpit in precisely the same manner, or rolls up his sleeves when he gets down to real pulpit-work just like the Esteemed Master.

The church which the disciple serves observes precisely the same order of service as that of the Leader. It sings the same narrow batch of favourite hymns and songs. It prays for the same things in the same words.

Close your eyes during the service, especially during the sermon, and you can finish some of the acolyte's sentences. The same intonations, the same sentence structure, the same applications ... he is little more than a replica of the Great Leader. It is not so much a matter of passing the baton as creating a replicant.

Mentors and models

Of course, it is natural and even proper for a man who is often in your orbit to develop some of your characteristics. Under healthy circumstances, a young man might particularly grow to emulate some of your particular strengths. Perhaps there are areas of theological study in which you are adept, or spheres of pastoral labour in which you excel. You might expect to be able to make some particular investments in these areas.

However, a man under your sway might also accrue

some of your distinctive weaknesses. Perhaps you struggle in some areas of theological understanding, possessing only a narrow or shallow capacity, and are not able to direct or encourage study in that region. Perhaps you are a limited preacher, or you struggle to give clear pastoral counsel, or you find face-to-face evangelism a great burden. Perhaps there is some constitutional weakness which he might unthinkingly imbibe—excessive sentimentality or harshness. Perhaps it is wise, under such circumstances, to call in others to help, or to send the man out into other environments. Encourage him to cultivate his own particular strengths to counteract what you cannot give him.

There is likely to be a natural replication of strengths and weaknesses, even with such care. Nevertheless, the main point is this: it is wrong to demand and pursue a wrong kind of shallow duplication. There is a danger of trying to reproduce yourself in the wrong way. This can be seen both in men and in churches: unless the disciple, and, in due course, any congregation he serves, matches the precise template that the master established, it is not considered faithfulness. This is not so much to play the role of the mentor as to insist upon the place of the guru.

Leaving aside the tendency of the younger man to

emulate the older, it is imperative that the mentor should cultivate a wise and humble graciousness. We ourselves need to be able to distinguish between what is of first importance and what belongs to personal preference, and we will want to make that plain in our teaching and training. While we must identify and insist on what is fundamental and essential, we should not make it our goal simply to reproduce ourselves in an artificial fashion. We desire children, not clones! We must be willing to allow those into whom we pour ourselves to grow, to become everything they are and could be, under God. We cannot force them to be another version of ourselves, or relentlessly hammer them into whatever shape we think they should be.

Perhaps most importantly, we must be willing for those whom we serve in this way to outgrow us. We trust that they will develop beyond us at the points where the Lord has given to them something he may not have granted to us. Our responsibility is not to produce little replicas, but rather to nurture whatever it is that God has made that man under our care. If there is any substance to the assertion that preaching is the communication of truth through personality, then we must allow that personality to be the legitimate filter through which the truth passes. We should not unrighteously impose our own personality, or any other, on another man.

7
A sacrificial investment

If we are truly seeking to pass the baton in this way, there will be many sacrifices which the mentor must make. It is only with sacrifice that it is possible to commit to other faithful men the things which you yourself have heard from faithful men (2 Tim. 2:2). We need to be ready for this. If we are going to build a tower, we need to work out how much it will cost, from the foundation up (Luke 14:28–30).

Time

You will have to sacrifice time. A man calls you and assures you that he just needs five minutes of your time. You will have to tell him, first, that he doesn't (he needs more), and second, that it doesn't matter (because you are willing to give more). After an hour he apologises to you for taking up too much of your time. You may have to let him know that you will certainly tell him when you believe that is the case. However, until you tell him that, he is free to use what you offer. Your investment of your time, you will say, is your business, and you are currently choosing to invest it in him.

Energy

You will have to sacrifice energy. All of this is done over and above the ordinary pastoral life. There will be moments of deep sighing, times when you really do not feel like pouring yourself out in ministry, seasons when you are disappointed or frustrated, periods when you wonder if it is worthwhile or all a grand waste of time. There will be occasions when you wonder how you are going to fit it all in. There will be points at which you feel washed out and have to stir your soul to do what you have committed to do, contrary to your present sense of what you have to offer.

Money

You will have to sacrifice money. You might have to travel to spend time together with the man under your care. You might need to eat and drink together. You might need to provide him books. You might have such books from your own mentors, with their names in the front, perhaps even with their notes in the margins.

Perhaps it is a particular gift, lovingly marked, 'To so-and-so, from so-and-so, with such-and-such.' There may be books that you have lovingly collected which he now needs more than you. You might need to set him up and help him out on various levels. You may have to open your home to put a roof over his head and your food cupboards to keep his stomach full. You may need to recalibrate the church budget—including your own salary—to help provide all or part of an income for someone.

Opportunity

You will have to sacrifice opportunity when you set out to pass the baton. You may not yet realise that it can be very painful, especially for a man who loves his labour, to give up opportunities for preaching and teaching. You are excited about that series of sermons on a certain book of the Bible. The regular ministry on a certain topic is one that has really gripped your soul. The evangelistic meetings that you have arranged are a wonderful new venture. The Bible studies or book studies you are working through are stimulating your own heart and doing good to others. While the work is hard, you would rather have more than fewer occasions to serve.

And now you need to step aside, at least at certain points. You need to vacate the pulpit from time to time, to offer opportunities to the younger man that you would dearly love to take yourself. It is not your pride that makes this hard, I hope, but rather your own sense of calling and duty. You will need to step aside so that he can learn his craft and develop his capacities. You might not be able to do all of the things you would like to do because you have to do this well. You might have to watch someone else who does not (yet) do them as well as you. Your own 'profile' may reduce as you provide space for and promote the gifts of others.

Stature

You may have to sacrifice stature. There may be people who warm to him more than to you. You will listen to people into whom you have poured hours of ministry tell you what a gifted chap this other guy is, and how helpful they find his ministry. People who have been converted under his ministry might naturally gravitate to him as a spiritual father. You might see him start to be offered opportunities that you would have loved, or to which your prideful heart might inwardly insist you are properly entitled. His gifts might grow beyond yours, with a corresponding growth in what the world loves to call 'profile'. It might be as petty as struggling to watch the flock of Christ cluster round a Christlike man of gift and grace to whom their hearts are drawn. It might mean stepping aside to let a man of greater gift exercise that gift in some sphere, or even just watching the hits and views for his sermons climb beyond yours. It will be an opportunity to demonstrate that, in this too, you are willing that Christ should increase, and you should decrease (John 3:30).

Comfort

You will have to sacrifice comfort. There will be hard conversations if you are concerned about entrusting the truth to competent and faithful men. Some of those might be the toughest talks you have. At times you may tell a well-meaning but ill-equipped man that he is not cut out for the work upon which he has set his heart. You might sit down with a man to dissect his sermons because they are still shallow or misdirected, and see his shoulders droop or his teeth clench. You might have to do some late parenting, and explain to someone their lack of a decent work ethic, without which they will never cut it in the work of an under-shepherd. You might need to tell someone that unless they pull their finger out, they will relinquish all the opportunities that they have craved. You may have to explain the difference between desiring a profile before men and desiring a good thing in the office of an elder. You might need to tell someone whose wife craves his eminence that he and she cannot have it, precisely because he is not governing his own home well. You might need to rebuke someone for their harshness or arrogance or cowardice in public or private ministry. You will have conversations that make you feel physically sick just thinking about them, conversations in which you hope that the pouring sweat is not too visible, conversations after which you wake up the next day and find you have pulled muscles just from sitting still or holding yourself upright. You will have to deal with the fallout of faithfulness, and a determination to do what serves God's glory and the good of the church, rather than pandering to carnal appetites and pushy personalities.

Other sacrifices

You may have to sacrifice more as you seek to pass on the baton. There may well be disappointments along the way. Some of them may be distinctly bitter, even agonising. You spend hours working on something, helping to hone a sermon or polish some aspect of delivery, only to have the hapless fellow make a complete hash of something, or repeat the same awkwardnesses over again. I remember hearing a well-known preacher, a man with the kind of ministry and influence of which some dream, talk about the origins of his ministry as a teacher of other preachers. He had gathered around him a group of men who seemed willing and able to learn from him. They not only sat under his more public ministry but now enjoyed a more private investment. One morning he walked in among them, and greeted them cheerfully: 'Good morning, brothers!' One turned to him, and responded with real venom: '*We* are not your brothers!' I do not know how long he had already spent with them, how many hours he had poured into them. They turned around *en masse* and walked away, wanting nothing more to do with him. We can become self-protective under such circumstances, even on a smaller scale. We become weary of offering our back to the smiters. We have been stabbed too often before, and so we become accustomed to putting on the armour. Judas betrayed the Lord Jesus. Demas forsook the apostle Paul, having loved the world. There may well be disappointments, some devastating, along the way.

The disciple's sacrifices

But the man or men being mentored will also have to make certain sacrifices. They too must give time. The men who hope to take up the baton need to offer something over and above merely being there as part of the church body on the Lord's day, or at the midweek meetings. That will impose a certain burden on their wives and children, if they are family men. Actually, their ability to order their lives and their homes in such a way as to create capacity and manage the burden will be part of what commends them to you and to the church.

It will cost them energy. They will have to engage

their hearts at the beginnings and endings of long days, and through the course of busy weeks, and over extended seasons of time, to put in and get out something from the extras. They will arrive home tired at times from the mental and physical efforts of faithful ministry. These are not the men who are casually absent from the meetings of the church. These are not the men who consistently turn up late to your reading groups and your study sessions with another batch of excuses about why they have not done the reading or produced the preparation. They are more likely to be the men who ask, 'What should I read? To whom should I listen?' and who show the fruits of such investment.

It may cost them comfort, as they realise just how far they are from being what they want to be and need to be, and perhaps once thought themselves to be. Some of us doubtless remember stomach-churning conversations with someone who loved us enough to tell us truths about ourselves that we would rather not have heard.

It may cost them money. They will be buying the worthy volumes you carefully recommend. They may be trimming their work hours, cutting into their days off in order to prepare sermons or attend conferences. They may have to pass by promotions at work because they want to remain in the church, or decide that they need to make a priority of their theological studies at a particular point.

It will cost them suffering, too. Remember what the French exiles called the training in Geneva that Calvin provided for men who would be sent back to France to minister the truth: 'Calvin's school of death'. Do you remember Paul's syllabus for Timothy? The younger man 'followed my doctrine, manner of life, purpose, faith, longsuffering, love, perseverance, persecutions, afflictions, which happened to me at Antioch, at Iconium, at Lystra—what persecutions I endured' (2 Tim. 3:10–11). The life of the minister and the cost of ministry cannot be decorated or varnished. Men need to know what they are getting into. Timothy was exhorted to understand what was at stake for him, in the face of the desertions and defections that were characteristic of that season of Paul's ministry. The younger man would need to communicate the same spirit to other men who would themselves get the truth, guard the truth and give the truth. Do you have a school of death? At least, of death to self? Are we inculcating a readiness to serve, to prepare someone to give all that a man is and has for Christ?

The church's sacrifices

There is also a sacrifice for a church when seeking to

ensure the passing of the baton. The whole congregation has an interest and makes an investment. They will sacrifice time and energy. They will have to endure the apprentice's first efforts and early sermons. They will try not to look as if they are wincing and groaning when the whole machinery jars and shudders! Churches must give such men room to learn. They may have to listen to a number of sermons before the novice begins to find his feet.

'What did you think of that Bible study?'

'Not much!'

'Yes, he has a few issues to iron out before we give him another opportunity next month.'

'What, really?!'

'Yes. Really. Because this month is already a lot better than last month.'

One older pastor referred to the first effort of a younger man in the congregation for which he cared as turbo-preaching. Animated more by nervous energy than by anything else, the young brother managed to deliver about sixty minutes' worth of teaching in closer to ten minutes, finishing in a lather of sweat. What do you do with such a man? What does the congregation do? Conclude that he is not cut out for the work? Are we so sure? What if the next time he managed to trim it down and slow it down, so that he delivered a thirty-minute sermon in twenty minutes? That might be a vast improvement!

We may have to accept that there may be some weaker sermons some weeks. We will have to allow for some mistakes of judgment, perhaps more than our recognised pastors make. This is not to diminish the importance of the sermon or the danger of sustained weakness in the pulpit. It is, rather, to accept that—as with any man in any pulpit—not every sermon is going to raise the roof. Some will be as ordinary as any man faithfully declaring the Word of God can be.

The church will be making a financial investment, appreciating that this is part of the work that the pastor will do with his time. There may be a training fund. From this a church might provide books or software or other material for the aspiring teachers and preachers, or help to provide other tools or opportunities for study or whatever else may be required. This might be a bookshelf at home, or a place at an upcoming conference, or a supplement to their income to give them a day a week to read and to prepare, or a course of study at a seminary.

And then, when we have made all such investments, and they have taken the baton, we may well send them away to invest what they have received somewhere else. We might think that this is all about the strength and the future of our local church. That is not necessarily the case. Do you notice the pattern of Paul? He is usually sending away his best men, sometimes temporarily, in some cases permanently. Even when he calls them back to himself, it is usually because he has something else for them to do. Suppose that you had two or three good men, with the increasingly evident capacity to serve as pastor-teachers in the church. Some distance away there is a struggling cause or a needy village, town or region. Do you send your least competent man? Do you ditch the one who would not be too badly missed, or do you send the most competent man because—under God—he is best equipped to accomplish something? Paul was a sacrificer. That is why he is writing to Timothy in Ephesus. That is why he is calling him back in order to be sent out again.

After all, Paul has seen something of this in his own experience. When the church in Antioch had reached a certain point, there were certain prophets and teachers, including Paul (then still known as Saul). As those five men 'ministered to the Lord and fasted, the Holy Spirit said, "Now separate to Me Barnabas and Saul for the work to which I have called them." Then, having fasted and prayed, and laid hands on them, they sent them away' (Acts 13:2–3). There seems little doubt that they sent away two of their best and brightest, without necessarily stripping the home church of what they genuinely required.

Paying the price

There is no-one involved in this passing of the baton who does not have to pay a price somewhere. We need to sign up to a costly investment, and we need to explain to the men in whom we invest that there will be a cost to them of comfort, ease, time, energy and money. We are not calling them to an effortless path, but inviting them to become labourers in the kingdom of God. The language of such labour is the language of agricultural endeavour, and military service, and athletic competition. It is all hard, sweaty, agonising, dangerous effort. The crop, the victory, the crown are often a long way in the distance. It is why we need trustworthy men. We need men who will keep ploughing and sowing though as yet there seems little prospect of reaping. We need men who will keep fighting the good fight though the crown is still to come. We need men who will keep running with endurance the race that is set before them, looking unto Jesus as the author and finisher of their faith.

8
An urgent investment

When did you start investing in your own redundancy? How long do you think you have to live? Is there a danger you will soon lay down the baton, no longer able to hold it and not having been able to pass it on?

I started thinking about and planning for my own redundancy within months of being appointed a pastor. In my best moments, I honestly think it would be something of an achievement if the congregation which I serve soon reached the point at which it would be able to say, 'We think that the time might have come for you to move on.' It is not that I necessarily want them to say that, or want them to want to say that! Neither am I itching to be put out to pasture. But I do want them, in principle, to be able to say, 'We have men who can continue this work, and perhaps you should move on to serve somewhere else.' Or what if they said, 'Look, an old warhorse like you can hold the fort here, but we should get this young man out into the field—you are an average man, he is a man who excels'? Would that count as a sign of ministerial success? Might we not count it as a blessing when our protégés overtake us? We are back in Antioch with Barnabas, Simeon, Lucius of Cyrene, Manaen and Saul (Acts 13:1). Who will stay and who will be sent?

A war footing

Timothy is going to move on from Ephesus. The very letter in which Paul urges him to pass on what he has learned to others in their turn is the letter in which he calls Timothy to come to him. He is reminding Timothy that neither of them have much time. Paul is being poured out like a drink offering (2 Tim. 4:6). Timothy's opportunities are quickly sliding past. The whole setting is of a church on a war footing, in a hostile and fast-paced environment. This is not pastoral labour in the sense of idyllic rural fields full of waving grain in golden light. This is the fluid and unstable battleground on which Paul and Timothy are contending for the souls of men.

In many parts of the world, and in many churches, Christians may feel as if we are on the back foot. Think of the area in which the Lord has placed you. How much gospel light is there? Consider the churches of the region. How much true preaching is there? How many of the faithful churches are thriving? How many have single elders or soon-to-retire men? Has the whole city or region heard the gospel? How many villages and towns have never heard the gospel, much less had an opportunity of consistent gospel ministry? There is no-one they know to ask about the hope of salvation. They would not know where to go or to whom they could turn if their souls were stirred. Some ministers' fellowships are populated largely by faithful men who have served steadily, often for decades. Those men gather, look around and see no-one coming through. The numbers dwindle as minds fail and bodies crumble.

Perhaps most grievously, the finest men some of us have known—our own models and mentors—are passing from the scene. For some of us, those esteemed men are now old, and we are already older than when they invested in us. We ourselves are no longer the young men. What is happening behind us? Many old ministers are now being poured out as drink offerings. They are on the last lap of the long race of service; to whom will they pass the baton?

Dropping the ball

There are churches that are struggling, and some are making desperate, even foolish decisions. Some of them have never thought about this matter of succession until the day that the leading light goes dark. The one man they might have asked for advice has been taken from them. Perhaps they have few contacts or counsellors. Some just start up a rotation of occasional preachers who will do no more than keep a gathering's head above water, for who knows how many years? They might hope that one of the visiting preachers would be acceptable enough for the church to take a gamble. They might hope that those two weeks of sermons he brought to them will not prove to be the only decent things he has prepared in two years. They might be in danger of being dazzled by a pleasant personality, a handsome face, an easy manner, a velvet voice. They do not dig down to the substance of a man's character, competence and capacity.

Some churches send out an alert to a denomination or organisation and leave the matter in their hands. Those who are calling the shots often have no real knowledge of the congregation. Perhaps they have their own agenda, sometimes even seeming happy to let some little cause run down so that they can sell the property and swell the coffers. Some do not know how to keep a well-meaning (or even officious and self-important) central officer from running the show remotely. Some place an advert in evangelical journals or newspapers and get a trickle of freelancers offering their doubtful services.

Preparing the church

At the very least, we should be equipping a congregation to be able to identify the kind of men whom the Lord is equipping and calling to shepherd the flock. If you are a pastor, and the Lord called you home suddenly, is the church prepared to act wisely and well? Who would righteously take the lead? Who already grasps the truth sufficiently well to hold things on the right course? Who knows where the church stands? The future of the church cannot hang on one heart and mind. We need trustworthy men who are proven and ready to carry this forward.

We cannot dawdle in our praying and doing. We cannot simply sit and wait for something to happen. Taking into account our limitations, we must begin to press this matter at the throne of grace, and to do all we can to carry out our duty wherever the Lord has put us.

9
A long-term investment

Passing the baton is an urgent investment because we need to begin today. It is a long-term investment because we will not finish tomorrow. It is an urgent investment that will not bring immediate returns. This is part of the sacrifice. It is something we carry out over the long haul. It cannot be completed in a few weeks. It will not be over in a few months. It will sometimes take years, at the very least, to prepare someone to carry the baton of fruitful ministry.

Finding a Timothy

Perhaps it is that little boy, whose dad is not even converted, but whose faithful mum is teaching him the Word of God. Or perhaps it is the grandson whose faithful grandparents look after him every week for an hour or so, teaching him the truth and praying for him fervently. Perhaps it is the quiet child who delights in truth from an early age. Perhaps he becomes that lad who has been holding his course at school as the pupils and teachers have bullied and teased him because he actually believes what the Bible says. Perhaps it is the boy who blossoms after conversion and begins reading for the first time in his life, and discovers an appetite and aptitude for theology. Perhaps it is the young man who can be found discussing the sermon he has just heard with his friends at church, and pressing home the truth. Perhaps it is the fellow whose family could never afford university, if they even thought of it, but who eagerly devours any books that you give to him. Perhaps it is the guy who struggles to read more than a paragraph or two, but who savours every word that proceeds from the mouth of the Lord and his faithful servants. Over time he proves that he can process it and profit by it, and has a knack for easy and clear communication.

And, at some point, you might say, 'I think we have a Timothy!' How long did that take? Five years? Ten? Eighteen? Twenty-five? And that may be only to reach the beginning of the more definite and deliberate process of formation into a man of God who can, in due course, teach others also.

Most of these investments take more years than months, some even decades, to come to full fruition. Furthermore, we should be thinking of a cycle of investment. We should not just be looking for the next man. We should be seeking the next men, and the men after them. We are looking down through the coming generations, and labouring and praying for those who will come after us, and those who will come after them.

Going over the ground

In this sense, it could also be considered a repeated investment. You spend a couple of years dealing with one man. Then you find that there are another two or three who are interested in following the same course. But you cannot just replicate it. The dynamics have changed. You adapt, you develop, while still covering the same kind of ground. Perhaps someone asks you if they can bring along a friend who wants to know more. We want someone who will be ready to stand in our place, and other places, when we are long gone, and tell other people the truth as it is in Jesus. Hopefully, the men in whom you have invested have gone on to invest in others also. The ripples are spreading! More men are being raised up to be preachers and teachers!

Many modern economic theories are selfish to the core. They maintain a here-and-now attitude. They presume that you will want to blow everything in the moment, to accumulate for yourself and then spend on yourself. Spiritual realities must be different. We are not fighting only for ourselves, but on behalf of those who will come after us. We have an inheritance to pass down. We have something to bequeath to those who follow us: the truth that saves, the truth that establishes, the truth that forms a people for the praise of the glory of God. That begins in the congregations that we serve.

The longer term

What is your long-term desire for the church which you serve? For how many generations do you hope there will be a bright and shining light where you are? Are we simply content to die in harness? What about those who follow? What about the other town and villages? What about the next neighbourhood? Consider the New Testament dynamics. Capernaum was not a large city. There were not tens of thousands of people in any of the ordinary towns and villages of the New Testament record. Some of the towns we live in could sustain tens of churches, if we agreed that we would each concentrate on only five or ten thousand souls!

What about the places we drive past? What about the regions and counties where the Lord has put us? Who will go? Who will reach people with the gospel after we have gone? In whom are we investing so that for generations to come, under God, there are men who are burning and shining lights in their generation? Where will new churches be planted? Who will pastor them? Who will care for the people who are now being converted, showing themselves God's means of bringing them from spiritual infancy to spiritual maturity? Who will soon be saying, 'We are identifying potential elders among our converts, and we are passing on to them the deposit of truth, so that they in due turn can pass it on to others'?

We talk about 'unreached people groups'. Most of us have unreached people groups right on our doorsteps. Within ten minutes of where most of us live and serve there are people who may never have heard the gospel, have never yet been willing to hear the gospel. Who will go to them? We must answer this question now, for the generations to come.

We cannot be so super-spiritual about this that we presume upon the ends without the employment of the means. Do we say, in effect, 'God will take care of it; that's his job'? God said to Paul, 'Go and preach the gospel.' As part of that, Paul took a Timothy under his wing, and said to him, 'You take others under your wing': 'the things that you have heard from me among many witnesses, commit these to faithful men who will be able to teach others also' (2 Tim. 2:2).

10
A shared investment

We seem to have an instinctive institutionalisation when it comes to answering such questions as the ones we have been considering. We demand specialised and professional baton-passers! In the New Testament, the church is the one institution established for the whole work of the kingdom, but there are some things that do not belong to the local church. Institutions may be needed to carry out work, even distinctly Christian work, that are not the remit of the local church, and which do not tread on its toes. However, it is amazing what kind of exegetical gymnastics are performed to validate the idea of a 'school of the prophets' in the New Testament. (Even that presumes that we know what was happening in 1 Samuel 19:18–24 and in 2 Kings 2 and

4:38–44, and that we should expect a precise and formal new covenant counterpart.) What would this even look like? What might it involve?

There are also some interesting interpretations of 2 Timothy 2:2 which effectively inaugurate Timothy as the first seminary professor of the New Testament. I cannot see that in the text. There are those who take this view of Paul in Ephesus. Acts 19:8–10 tells us that the apostle

> … went into the synagogue and spoke boldly for three months, reasoning and persuading concerning the things of the kingdom of God. But when some were hardened and did not believe, but spoke evil of the Way before the multitude, he departed from them and withdrew the disciples, reasoning daily in the school of Tyrannus. And this continued for two years, so that all who dwelt in Asia heard the word of the Lord Jesus, both Jews and Greeks.

'Aha!' we are told. 'There you have it! A university course in theology, with none less than an apostle as the instructor!' It is sometimes presented as more or less a seminary degree. Again, that reads into the text something that is not there in full and perhaps not even in part.

The church at the centre

If we are to be faithful to our Bibles, the answer is not

a thoughtless recourse to institutions other than the church for the entirety of the church's preparation of its future teachers. What we do have to recognise is that there are few men and few churches who have the gifts and resources, in isolation from one another, to do all that we have discussed.

In some respects, our answers to this question may depend on our ecclesiology. I am a Baptist Congregationalist, or an Independent Baptist. I see a danger of churches which profess independency becoming isolationist in practice. Not all embrace that communion between churches—involving mutual communication, connection, contribution and cooperation—by which the kingdom of God thrives. Where churches have real common ground, there is scope for us to work together to this end. Some churches have little capacity for providing or securing seminary training, even if they wished to pursue it. Some seem to have assumed that the responsibility for training preachers and teachers is a professorial rather than a pastoral role. I readily confess that my solutions sit within my convictions as a churchman. As we have already seen, that is not to say that a faithful seminary is not part of the solution to the need for training a man, either sending him to another place or using the resources a seminary may supply. In some cases, it may be near the whole of the solution. But always the man who is learning to serve must be among faithful saints and under the care of faithful pastors in a local church. Never does that absolve a sending church of its responsibilities or duties, or allow any seminary to supplant the local church and its functions.

Putting it into practice

What might all this look like for pastors and churches who want to embrace this responsibility of passing the baton as instructed by the Word of God? In 1 Timothy 3:2 and Titus 1:9 there is a quality that is required of every elder. Each one must be able to teach. I would make a distinction between teaching and preaching. All preaching is teaching, but not all teaching is preaching. There are different modes and channels of instruction which lie within that overarching expectation of aptitude to teach. Some of that may be more intellectual or academic in its character.

Another thing to take into account is that while every elder must be able to teach, there are some men within the eldership who clearly have distinct gifts with regard to teaching and preaching. Paul can distinguish between elders within a particular church, it would seem: 'Let the elders who rule well be counted worthy of double honour, especially those who labour in the word and doctrine'

(1 Tim. 5:17). All the elders are ruling, but some of them are ruling well. Among those who are ruling, and ruling well, there is a further group who 'labour in the word and doctrine'. They deserve a particular reward, just as those who rule well deserve a particular reward.

The point is that even within the eldership of a particular congregation, righteous distinctions can be made in terms of the graces and gifts that can be identified. How much more when you survey the elderships of various congregations? Everything you read in the New Testament about the organic, dynamic nature of new covenant church life pushes us in this direction. There are believers who have different 'talents'. God has bestowed upon them different gifts in different measures for investment in his heavenly kingdom. Paul could say that by the grace of God he was who and what he was. He could distinguish himself from the other apostles in their experiences, gifts and responsibilities.

Within the church, and among the churches, and among those who are appointed to care for and rule over the church, we can expect varieties of grace and gift, of competence and capacity. Even in the New Testament it is clear that some churches have particular strengths and weaknesses. There are churches which need a Titus or a Timothy in order to address certain challenges. Crete is Titus's costly reward for his growing ability to handle a difficult situation! There is a measure of sanctified common sense in some of these distributions and directions.

Without reading too much into the tired theme of a fearful Timothy, is it not possible that Paul thought that Titus was better suited to Crete? At the same time, I don't imagine we look at Ephesus and think that pastoral life there would be an easy ride. Is there something of a 'horses for courses' process in the apostolic oversight that is not unspiritual, but actually a function of Spirit-filled and prayerful church government?

Here is one of our challenges. We may know of organisations and institutions that produce a stream of candidates for ministry. The raw materials are fed into an institutional conveyor belt. The handle of academic process turns, and the product rolls off the line. Few seem to pause and ask whether the apparent efficiency of the process is a sufficient reason for us to try to replicate the model. If there is any suggestion of failure, we might be tempted to adapt D. L. Moody's famous response to the person who told him, 'I don't like the way you evangelise.' Moody replied, 'Well, I like the way I evangelise far better than the way you don't evangelise.' Who are we to critique others who are doing something when we seem to be doing little or nothing? And so we set out to do something similar.

At the other end of the scale, are some churches in danger of simply hoping that somehow the Holy Spirit will make everything instantly and painlessly better? We neglect to use God's means in order to accomplish God's ends, and call ourselves spiritual people because of it.

Holy cooperation

We have some clear patterns in the Word of God, and alongside of those some variables of which we need to take account. Given all this, how can any one church, or a number of churches connected to and cooperating with one another, make the kind of investments that Paul calls Timothy to make, committing the deposit of apostolic truth to faithful men who will be able to teach others also (2 Tim. 2:2)? This should be a product of healthy churches of healthy faith with healthy leaders engaging in the healthy teaching of healthy Christians.

We should accept that there may be limits to the level of cooperation that might be possible. That might depend on the convictions of the people involved. If you have different definitions of 'church', then this kind of labour will be hard to pursue together. How could a church send a man to and support him in a programme which did not share that church's most basic convictions about God and his kingdom?

Not every congregation has all that is required for the whole process. But suppose there is one church which has several gifted men with a manifestly developing aptitude for the work of ministry. Another congregation has a measure of financial security, even relative wealth. Another has a very gifted pastor-teacher, with a number of elders and perhaps other members who are theologically astute and able to teach to a particularly deep and detailed degree. Another church has some excellent evangelists among the eldership. Another congregation has a growing congregation but an older eldership, including a recently retired minister, with a thriving evangelistic outreach in a nearby neighbourhood.

How could those churches labour together in order to meet the opportunities? Note, too, that we must go beyond mere needs in order to embrace real opportunities. Is there not some way of combining the resources, capacities and demands of those churches in order to make the most of everything that they have?

Suppose that from among the gifted men in the first church, one is a superb communicator but not a great scholar. Another is a real 'brainiac' with an unusual aptitude for learning and a high-level capacity for high-level communication. A third is a natural evangelist. How does that change things? We should not assume that the scholar needs more scholarship. Perhaps he needs a spell on the streets to ground his learning. He might profit from some time with a real preacher to help him learn how to speak to ordinary people. Perhaps the great mind will never actually be a good preacher, but he might become an outstanding teacher. Perhaps the evangelist needs some theological grounding to equip him for the work to which he is naturally inclined. Perhaps the easy communicator without the academic turn of mind needs some encouragement from a seasoned elder.

Putting down roots

It might be that one or more of these men would profit from a more academic course of instruction. We might certainly ask the question, 'Are there institutions which might equip some or all of these men for the work the Lord may be calling them to do?' However, that should not necessarily be our default response and our inevitable decision. It is within the church that these things need to be worked out and played out.

Too many men are ripped from the very

soil in which they have been growing, maturing and beginning to bear fruit, and placed in an environment which then prevents or at least undermines the very growth you have been seeing. The intention was that this man might grow more; the effect might be that his growth is stunted or twisted. Let us also remember that academic attainment is not the same as intellectual rigour or practical ability. Some men have their seminary degree but have clearly never thought anything through or come to any kind of settled convictions. They present as mere parrots with prodigious memories, but no real intelligence of their own. Some would-be pastors are like men who have earned some kind of veterinary degree without ever touching an animal. They are all theory and very little practice. And some men who have turned their backs on seminary training seem to take pride in ignorance, as if a decision not to pursue a more academic course is some kind of excuse for intellectual laziness and shallowness.

Thinking it through

Churches, individually and in communion with each other, need to think this through. It is the responsibility of the church to train its future leaders. How could we, given these challenges and opportunities, use God's appointed means to accomplish God's appointed ends?

What does it mean for a church, and for churches in communion with one another? Churches need to recognise that even delegated responsibility is still real responsibility.

Besides, even small beginnings can bring great rewards eventually. What if you only have one man, and he is used of the Lord? What if a church planted then works with the church which planted it, so that two churches are now investing in the same work in which one was engaged before? What scope might there be over time for real development and extended cooperation?

11
A beneficial investment

It may sound as if this responsibility to pass the baton is all a great burden for the elders or elder of any particular church. It may sound as if it is costly for the church as a whole. It is certainly a great responsibility, but it is a responsibility that brings with it genuine blessings to those who engage in it.

Productive pressures

This work benefits the man passing on the baton as well as the man being trained. When a pastor takes another man or men under his wing, it sharpens and develops his own thinking and working. He becomes more conscious of the need to model what it means to serve the Lord. He knows that he is to call others to imitate him just as he also imitates Christ (1 Cor. 11:1). In this, he is further stimulated to walk before God and his people in a way which can be followed. If he is to pass the baton to another man, he needs to show him how to run with it.

It adds a new dimension and a distinct focus to some of his pastoral labours. He will be reading different books, or perhaps reading books in a different way, or reading old books with a new purpose. As he considers what it means to make this investment, he will find new insights into the Word of God. There may be some distinct areas of study that he undertakes in order to equip himself for the work. He will become more aware of the weaknesses of his own learning.

He will become more alert to the points in his own sermons in which he has not handled the Word of God as carefully or clearly as he might have done. When he talks through the issues of hermeneutics, exegesis and homiletics,[1] he will be happily obliged to delve deeper into the Scriptures. He must consider whether or not he properly applies to himself the principles he is cultivating in others. He will answer questions which may demand more careful thought about his own principles and practices than

1 The disciplines of interpreting and understanding, explaining, and teaching and applying the Word of God.

previously, or draw out depths of understanding which he had never before required.

His praying should be both developed and enriched as it envelopes a new dimension of his work. He may have to instruct in fields of theology where he himself has been either woolly or ignorant. This will oblige him to develop a simple, straightforward and systematic appreciation of the truth which had before eluded him or never been required of him. In order to teach, he will be required to learn.

Under God, it may even prove that he is himself kept on the straight and narrow path by engaging with those distinct aspects of the work, either in the more general sense of diligent commitment, or the more specific challenges of error or sin that might undermine his work or even disqualify him from office. There may be moments when the fact that others are looking up to him and watching him may be a God-given help in keeping from certain transgressions.

The joy of the work

There is joy in entrusting others with the truth. There may prove to be the joy of seeing continuity of gifted and responsible leadership of the church. There is the joy of developing ministerial friendships as—over time—the teacher and the disciple could become comrades and fellow-labourers. There is the joy of seeing seed sown bearing fruit, of steady effort producing eventual maturity. There is the joy of seeing men uncover areas of gifts and strength which you yourself lack. There is the joy of seeing particular sheep of Christ growing in grace and knowledge. There is the joy of seeing the whole church well-fed and well-led. There is the joy of seeing Christ honoured in the recognition and appreciation of his gracious gifts to his church.

The blessings are there for the whole church, too. As the congregation invests in a particular man or men, they are nourished by the truth which such men preach and teach. They may obtain a richer and more varied diet of ministry, or profit from a different emphasis or the employment of specific gifts. They may be stretched by new opportunities that open up. They will have the joy of seeing young people who have grown up in the church blooming into men of God with a willingness and ability to serve in the church in various ways. There is the potential blessing of united and sustained pastoral ministry, as men of like mind and varied gift labour together for the care of the flock, not just for a few years but over generations. There is the joy of embracing the fact that Christ sends out labourers into the harvest field, and being the means to that end.

We should not imagine that all the rewards of this work are deferred to the glory to come. The full weight of them might only be known in the new heavens and the new earth. The foretaste of them begins much sooner. Paul was happy at the prospect of a visit to Rome, that he might 'be encouraged together with you by the mutual faith both of you and me' (Rom. 1:12). Paul was eager to see his son in the faith when all others deserted him (2 Tim. 4:9–10). It is by no means wrong to anticipate that this investment will prove likewise sweet to those who engage in it.

12
A Christlike investment

I hope you have seen that passing the baton is fundamentally a Christlike investment. I trust that has been clear by implication throughout this brief book. Let me now make it explicit. Passing the baton of ministry may be one of the most Christlike elements of any man's service.

Christ made this additional investment as part of his service here upon earth. From very early on, he was labouring to prepare labourers for the harvest field. It was a selective investment, for he prayerfully chose the Twelve to be with him, and spent time teaching them by instruction and example. His was a deliberate investment. It was often incidental but never accidental. He often took his disciples aside to teach them, or gave them seasons of instruction that they might, by the help of his Spirit, understand the Scriptures.

Christ made a personal investment. He spent three years or so with those men, moving around the country so that they could receive from him all that he was able to give them. It was a gracious investment, in every possible sense. Likeness to Christ was the great goal, in doctrine, devotion and deed, but that never eradicated the personality of those who followed him. Eventually, each could come to say, 'Imitate me, just as I also imitate Christ' (1 Cor. 11:1).

It was a sacrificial investment. How much it cost our Lord to serve in this way! He died for those men, having already come into the world for them. He had lived alongside them, and shown them over the time he spent with them that he was modelling the kind of service that they too must render: 'For I have given you an example, that you should do as I have done to you' (John 13:15). It was an urgent investment, for the Lord laboured under a sense that his time was short. There was much to be done, a sense of urgency that communicated itself to his disciples in their sense of pressure to carry out the work while it is day. It was a long-term investment. After Christ ascended, he left his disciples with the commission to 'go … and make disciples of all the nations, baptising them in the name of the Father and of the Son and of the Holy Spirit'. They were to teach the disciples to observe all things that he had commanded them. He gave them the promise, 'Lo, I am with you always, even to the end of the age' (Matt. 28:19–20).

His investment was to roll down through the generations, and in that sense was to be a shared investment, picked up by each succeeding generation. Each in turn has committed the things that they have heard from their mentors 'among many witnesses ... to faithful men who will be able to teach others also' (2 Tim. 2:2). And Christ still prays for his church. It has never ceased to be a prayerful investment.

13
A prayerful investment

This work of passing on the divine deposit of apostolic truth can never be accomplished apart from believing prayer. Christ himself urged his disciples, 'The harvest truly is great, but the labourers are few; therefore pray the Lord of the harvest to send out labourers into His harvest' (Luke 10:2). Christ himself, time and again, is found in prayer at those seminal moments when his disciples will be chosen, instructed and commissioned. He prays still for his people, that they might be with him where he is, and that means he prays for blessing upon the means of grace that he himself has given.

What does that signify for churches and their elders? It means that we must make prayer for future generations of pastor-teachers regular and earnest components of our public intercessions. This should be a prominent feature of our Sunday services, our prayer meetings, our private devotions. It might involve at least the following elements.

How to pray

We should plead that the Lord would raise up this breed of faithful men. We might pray that the children of the church would have among them future elders. We could ask that from among the current membership we might find some men who are growing in grace and in the knowledge of Christ in a distinct way, men who will soon be able to begin serving in new ways.

We should pray that the Lord would bring in such men. We might pray that there would be women of God who are fitted to become wonderful helpers suited by God to the men whom they will support and alongside whom they will serve. We pray that those who are being converted but who will never be elders might be able to discern what real ministry looks and sounds like, and how it can be encouraged, supported and appreciated.

It is more than possible—under present circumstances, entirely likely—that the next generation of pastor-preachers is yet to be converted. Many of them, if not most, may be yet to hear the good news. We ought to be pleading with God that the gospel we preach, and the testimony of the church to the saving power of God, would be his means of converting sinners. We ought further to pray that there would be new brothers who begin to ask, in the light of the mercies of God, what it would mean for them to present their bodies as a living sacrifice, holy and acceptable to God, which is their reasonable service (Rom. 12:1). We should pray that there would be some who are so gripped by these new realities that it seems almost inevitable to them that they should go and preach the Christ who has saved them from their sins.

We should pray that the Lord would work through the investments of any church, and churches in communion with each other, to equip and enable such called men. We should pray for great wisdom for those who make those investments in a particular way. We want them to be able to say with Paul that these pastors and preachers in training 'have carefully followed my doctrine, manner of life, purpose, faith, longsuffering, love, perseverance, persecutions, afflictions ... what persecutions I endured' (2 Tim. 3:10–11). We must be pleading with heaven for heaven's blessing on such labours, that we might send out men formed and informed by the Word of God.

And that is the next stage. We should pray that the Lord would send out these labourers into the harvest field. We should not be hoarding but investing our riches. Arrows are of no real use if they remain always stored in the quiver, or even poised on the string. Sooner or later Christ's soldiers must march to war. Such a moment is costly and risky. We are sent out 'as sheep in the midst of wolves', needing to be 'wise as serpents and harmless as doves' (Matt. 10:16). There comes a time when the men who have matured under such mentoring will need to be commissioned. Some may serve at home, others will be sent out, some into far-flung places, each to honour God in all that they do and say. We should pray for such a time.

And we should continue to pray that the Lord would use well his willing servants. We must pray that he would equip them, uphold them, enable them, sustain them and bless them. We must pray that he would keep them faithful and make them fruitful. A church's responsibility does not end when her spiritual sons step out on to the battlefield. We need to continue praying for them. We must plead for their spiritual preservation in a hostile environment. We must seek from heaven the courage they need to go on speaking the truth as it is in Jesus, and living and dying so as to hear from their Lord those precious words, 'Well done, good and faithful servant; you were faithful over a few things, I will make you ruler over many things. Enter into the joy of your lord' (Matt. 25:21).

Looking ahead

It is our reputation with Christ which really counts. The names of the current generation of pastors and preachers will soon be entirely forgotten. How long after we pass from this fading world will someone remember who we are? Is that a bit depressing? Maybe the people to whom we preach will remember us for a few years. Maybe a full generation of people might recall our labours. The chances are that people will not remember us. But that is not the point. It is not our name that they need to know. It is the name of Jesus Christ.

The best thing that we can do for those who follow us is to ensure that the baton is passed on to those who will be able to teach others also. They must stand where we stand, go where we have gone and where we have never been, to preach Christ, to make disciples, to teach all that our Lord has commanded us to know and to do.

It is good and right and necessary that we should consider these things. We must then act on the basis of our planning. Investments must be made, not merely discussed. We must step out in faith, depending on the answers to our prayers. In a sermon on Acts 13:49, entitled 'Gospel Missions', the inimitable Charles Haddon Spurgeon sent out a call for apostolic men to go about their work in an apostolic style backed up by apostolic churches and under an apostolic influence of the Holy Spirit.[1] It is that kind of desire that we need. It is that kind of hope that we must pursue.

The first question must be: 'Who is our man? Who are our men?' We must answer this question carefully and fairly. It might not be the men in their teens and twenties. Some may grow into this later in life as their gifts develop. Some men are converted later in life, and only then can they be considered for such a role. We need an eye focused by prayer to identify Christ's gifts to Christ's church.

If you are a church member, who are those men for whom the church prays and in whom the church invests? Each church needs to pray and to work to be a seedbed for the kind of labourers that will go out into all the world and preach the good news. If you are also a pastor, who are those developing men who are under your wing? Who is doing the extra work and putting in the hard yards? Who takes their

1 C. H. Spurgeon, 'Gospel Missions' in *The New Park Street Pulpit* (London: Passmore & Alabaster, 1856), 2:177 *ff*.

opportunities and responds to your feedback? Who comes along with you and learns from you?

When the Lord's voice is heard, saying as he did to Isaiah, 'Whom shall I send, and who will go for Us?' (Is. 6:8), let us pray that, in these days, there will be a generation of men gripped by divine grace. Let us pray for men growing and serving in churches which take seriously their responsibility to serve Christ in these things, who will say, humbly and prayerfully, 'Here am I! Send me.'

So what do we do next? I hope that the following counsels will help to those who are eager to give attention to this matter, but are not sure where to begin. In each case, I have tried to provide a skeleton, and put a little meat on the bones (drawing from the previous material) so you can work towards putting this into practice.

14
A pastoral responsibility

What should the elders of the churches be doing in order to pass the baton?

Pray

While we concluded our study above with prayer, I would advise to begin with it. As John Bunyan apparently said, 'You can do more than pray after you have prayed, but you cannot do more than pray until you have prayed.' Pray over what you have and what you lack. Pray over what you wish for and what you fear for. Pray for who you have and who you want or need. Lay the matter before God, not just for your own congregation, but for others you know. Pray for the kingdom of God in the nation where he has put you, and for its worldwide spread. Pray privately and publicly. Let your petitions be large!

Plan

Think about how you might begin to equip a man or men who emerged in your church as a potential elder or preacher. You do not necessarily need a formal course of study worked out. Nevertheless, it is wise to think how you might do this with different kinds of men, under different circumstances, with different kinds and degrees of gifts.

Some might be more scholarly, others more inclined to action. Some will be prodigious students, others will scrape along and force their way through a few words of reading or writing every week. You might have just one man, or you might have a group of men. Some might be teachers, one or two might be preachers. How will you serve them? What resources might you need? Think about the books they ought to read and the study courses they might take.

Remember that some will have more spare time, while others are gathering scraps of opportunity around other commitments. Some might do a lot with a little, working fast and on their own initiative. Others might be slow off the block, and need more spoon-feeding. Some might have the liberties and opportunities of single life, others the responsibilities and opportunities of marriage and families. Some might be much younger, and you may end up doing as much parenting as pastoring if they are teenagers or a little older, especially if they have had no Christian background. Some might be older, more mature in the faith, with late-flowering gifts and appetites.

In each case, give a few moments to think of how you would begin such a programme, how you might try to hold together all the possibilities for a range of men, or just the one or two. It might be difficult to do this in a vacuum. Turn your mind to the men you now have, if any, and turn them over in your mind. Do any of them manifest the kind of trustworthiness which commends itself? Remember that you are, in part, identifying and selecting men who are more likely to serve the church in particular ways in the future. Thinking about these particular men might help to make your planning a little more concrete and a touch more definite and substantial. Now the scheme is less vague, and you begin to see what particular resources might be required and employed for these particular men.

Consider, too, the avenues by which teaching and preaching gifts might be tested, and how this could be done to best advantage. Perhaps you need to make space in the schedule of ministry to give opportunity to particular men for teaching and preaching. That might be at different levels. Some might be teaching a Sunday school or Bible class for children or adults. Are there evangelistic opportunities on the streets and at the doors where some could develop an edge? You might appoint some to serve in some way on the Lord's day. Do you have an order of service that includes explaining and reading Scripture apart from the sermon? If so, this might be an opportunity for them to learn by studying, and to demonstrate what they are learning. Prayer meetings and Bible studies are also opportunities for men to step up. If you have no-one in the congregation who is willing or able to make such an investment at this point, perhaps you can open up those opportunities to men from other churches who need them.

Prepare

If your current capacity for the work is slim, begin to carve out or reserve some capacity for the kind of investment you would like to make. Hopefully, as you engage in the work, the capacity for it might expand as you have more people who are willing and able to help. For example, a few men who can preach occasionally might give you some scope to invest in one man who might in due course preach more regularly.

If you can, make budgetary preparations for

the support of men or the provision of necessary materials. It may be that you start laying up a stock of books or other media which you will use when the time comes. If the investment is imminent, you will need to start putting into immediate practice some of those plans described above with regard to balance of labour and opportunity.

You also need specifically to cultivate the spirit of patience and humility in service that will prepare you for the sacrifices you might make. It is hard to do this ahead of time, without realising quite what it might mean. You might need to accommodate the gifts of a less-experienced or even a less-gifted man. You might need to take on all the harder pastoral cases so that someone else can cut their teeth on the more straightforward situations. It might simply be a matter of making space in the schedule of public ministry for other men to learn, to develop, to spread their wings.

You also need to prepare the church. It may be other church officers who first of all need to understand and embrace the opportunities. However, because it will be a corporate task, in some measures, you will also need to lay it before the congregation. They need to know what is coming and how they will be involved. Of course, you would also need to speak to any particular men who are going to be involved, working through the possibilities and their willingness and ability to make the most of the opportunities that will come their way.

Pursue

What can you start doing now? Could you begin some reading or study groups at different depths of understanding and capacity? It may be as simple as taking someone with you when you go about certain aspects of pastoral business and ministerial labour. Perhaps you could visit some elderly members or some widows or widowers with one of the men in the church? You could take someone with you on a hospital visit. You could rope someone in to come out and knock on the doors of the neighbourhood with you. You might simply ask someone to come and spend some time in prayer with you.

If you cannot do some or all of this yourself yet, you might encourage or assist another man who is doing it. That might mean giving an opportunity to a man from another congregation who is learning the work of ministry. You can provide him with some encouragement and advice, and also feed back to the elders who are responsible for him. Perhaps you have time, especially if you are part of a healthily multiple eldership, to spend some hours with someone who could benefit from your particular expertise or experience? It might even be that you could help to support a man who needs financial assistance in order to further his studies. In return for this, he might be able to serve in some capacity, even occasionally.

At some point you will take the plunge and give a man more prominent opportunities to teach or preach. Then you will learn just what more you need to do by way of planning and preparing! But, as you have the opportunity, expose these brothers to a healthy range of healthy influences. Make sure that they engage with other wise men. Recommend, pass out and insist upon the reading of particular books or the watching of particular resources. Identify helpful fellowships or conferences where they will learn of what is going on outside their immediate circle, perhaps by being exposed to preachers of marked faithfulness or distinct gift (and, hopefully, both!). Make sure that they see the nitty-gritty of church life near and far so that they know what they are getting into.

And, if the work is slow, hard and disappointing, be assured that this is kingdom work, and is likely to be so in this fallen world. Do not give up! 'Cast your bread upon the waters, for you will find it after many days' (Ecc. 11:1). Keep casting it, and then wait in patient hope.

15
A congregational responsibility

I hope that these prospects excite you, if you are one of God's people. We need to bear in mind that the product is the result of a process. Too many Christians like certain products but dislike or resent certain processes. They appreciate the outputs, but are less keen on the inputs.

If we are to see men of God raised up for this and future generations of kingdom labour, we must ourselves be ready to engage in the processes which, under God, will produce such an outcome. We need to use God's means to accomplish God's ends, and to expect God's means to accomplish God's ends. So we need to ask about at least four things.

Your heart

Consider your heart. Are you willing to get involved and to get invested? Will you commit yourself, as a member of the congregation, to this work? You may not feel like you have much to contribute, but your eager and earnest engagement, your particular encouragements, will be worth their weight in gold. A congregation that is careless or resentful of the demands that this work places upon the whole body, and those who serve it as elders and deacons, will make this labour much harder and slower. It will become much more difficult, if not—humanly speaking—impossible. It is vitally important that the whole church (or, at least, a good portion of it) sees the significance of what is involved.

Your head

Your heart is unlikely to stay in the work unless your head is anchored to the work. The saints need to make a principled commitment to making the most of these opportunities. You will need to think about a great deal. Not least, you need to consider carefully the graces and gifts that the Lord has placed within his church. Give a patient and positive hearing to men who are starting out. Allow them to be who they are, what they are, when they are. Take care not to judge a man based on what he was five or ten years ago, failing to recognise that the Spirit may have worked much grace in him over the ensuing years.

You will also need to think not just about the men who do the work, but about the work that they do. This is a corporate responsibility, under the oversight of the elders. When you hear particular brothers teach or preach, you will need to do more than say, 'Oh, that was nice!' There needs to be a properly critical engagement, a real Berean spirit in which eager hearers search the Scriptures to see whether or not they have heard God's truth clearly and accurately and forcefully explained (Acts 17:11).

Be an eager and intentional listener when the men in development preach and teach, and give them helpful feedback. You could end up considering the best kind of training for a particular man or men. You need to make wise decisions with regard to each man. Is more formal training a good option? Are you in a position to support him in seminary? Are you able to send him to a reliable seminary or put him under some particular course of instruction? You will need to think about when and where and how particular gifts might be exercised or employed, both in the training phase and then in being sent by the church to work either nearer at hand or further afield.

Your hands

Your elders are going to need your hands—your active engagement. Perhaps you are one of those who seeks or should receive particular investments. Are you ready? We shall look at more of that below. Even if not, do not underestimate the contribution that you can make. For example, it may be that, in order for a pastor to take others under his wing, he needs some wing space! Can you help him by taking on work that he is currently doing but does not need to be doing? Can you relieve him of something which is essentially a distraction from his pastoral responsibilities so that he can pursue them, including this?

Consider also that there may be resources you have that can be invested in the work of the church. For some, it may be a matter of sustained or increased financial giving so that there is space in the budget to make this work. It may be an appropriate gift to a brother who needs a little help in order to make the most of his opportunities. For others, it may be a spare room in the house where a student could live. It could be providing a work space for a man who needs some peace and quiet, or somewhere to meet for a group of men studying together. If you have some measure of responsibility for the church budget as a deacon, are you shaping that budget to allow for this kind of investment?

Your hopes

Consider your hopes. Are you, eagerly and prayerfully

looking out for men of grace and gift who answer the descriptions above? If necessary, perhaps you could bring them to the attention of the elders? This is especially true if—for whatever reason—you may have seen something promising before others have done so.

You must continue to uphold the various workers before the throne of grace, both those training and those being trained, in order that they might be able to last the course. If the church is not yet engaged in this, could you suggest to the elders who lead the public prayers and arrange the meetings for prayer that this might go on the agenda?

Keep your eyes fixed on God, and go on looking to him for all that is needed in order to sustain the work of his kingdom. Do not become despondent and despairing! Christ knows how to take care of his flock. He gives gifts to his church when and where they are needed, so go on pleading with him for them and looking to him to provide them.

16
A personal responsibility

And what of the men being trained? What of the men to whom the baton is being passed? What about you?

Internal considerations

Are you the kind of man we have been talking about? It is no light thing to come to that conclusion, and you must do so both by yourself and with others: 'For I say, through the grace given to me, to everyone who is among you, not to think of himself more highly than he ought to think, but to think soberly, as God has dealt to each one a measure of faith' (Rom. 12:3).

You need to hold yourself up to the scriptural standards, to the full-orbed and richly coloured portrait of the man of God painted in the Bible. With that in mind, you should ask whether or not, or to what extent, you are fitting the template. In order to ask that question, you will need the counsels of your elders and other mature Christians. Bear in mind, too, that you might need the humility to hear the answer, 'No!' or, 'Not yet!'

Your own answer might be, 'I am not called to be an elder of the church.' It might be, 'I am not yet called or equipped to be an elder of the church.' Even if that is the case, I hope you would still ask, 'What can I do? Where can I serve?' Just because you cannot do everything does not mean that you can or should do nothing. Indeed, in the exercise of the gifts that you currently possess, more might develop or be uncovered.

Submit yourself to the elders of the church in the matter. Put yourself at their disposal. Ask for their input. It may be that they have never needed to think about these things before, and you might be the catalyst for their consideration and participation. Perhaps you must graciously get the matter on the agenda of the church.

In doing so, consider your track record as a worker generally and in the church. Think about whatever teaching, training, or employment you have had so far. The kind of work we have been discussing in this book is likely to demand more of you than you have ever needed to put in before. There is no space for lightweights and layabouts in Christ's ranks; his people are volunteers in the day of his power. 'If you have run with the footmen, and they have wearied you, then how can you contend with horses? And if in the land of peace, in which you trusted, they wearied you, then how will you do in the floodplain of the Jordan?' (Jer. 12:5). In other words, if you have no consistent pattern of diligence, reliability and responsibility in the work that you have done up to this point, do not assume that greater opportunity would automatically inspire you to step up. 'He who is faithful in what is least is faithful also in much; and he who is unjust in what is least is unjust also in much' (Luke 16:10).

Are you willing to learn? Will you make yourself willing to learn? This is not just about an outward show of humility. It is about being both willing and able to take to heart the counsels you will receive, and even some of the setbacks and delays that you might face. If you are setting yourself on the path of service, then you will be always learning, always striving, always being conformed to Christ. This will take place by the operations of the Spirit upon you and by means of your own responses to those operations and all that they involve.

I would urge you to count the cost and to consider the privilege. You may not have a great deal to offer, or feel that you do. Even if you are the working equivalent of the widow's two very small copper coins (Luke 21:1–4), give what you have, and you will receive the praise of Christ.

External preparations

If you have a heart for the work, and some encouragement from the church for it, then think about what you need to do by way of preparation. Some of these preparations might be or become more radical, either now or in the future. It may be a matter of finding a healthy church with faithful under-shepherds who will ask the right questions and seek the right answers. I know of a man who deliberately withheld his growing sense of a call to minister God's Word for some time. He knew that if he expressed such a desire in the church in which he then was, he would have been celebrated as another ministerial trophy, and thrust out ill-equipped and under-prepared for the work. Patience paid dividends!

Perhaps you will need to approach the elders of the church in which you currently serve to ask them to take you under their wing. You might ask for a reading list. Then you can begin to work your way through a series of key texts that will begin to equip you at a fundamental level for the kind of work you might do. You may not need to give up or change your current employment. However, you might need to ask what opportunities you might take or pass by in order to make the most of your chance to learn in the church. For some, that might be putting down roots in a local church rather than being promoted to somewhere lacking a sound church. For others, it might mean cutting away some of the waste in order to carve out some extra time and space in the schedule.

If you are married, talk this over with your wife. Is she willing and able to support you in this? If she is a maturing believer, she ought to be the first one with an opinion about your credibility and capacity. She is the one who, under God, will help to build the platform on which you stand to serve. If she is either not willing or able to release you, in measure, for the work, then that will have a massive impact on what you are able to do.

If you are not married, make this a part of your consideration. While none of us know all that the future holds, many a promising man has been held back or hindered in service because he has married unwisely. In some cases, of course, a providential hindrance might arise: sickness or weakness in the family might demand more of a man's energies than he had anticipated. But I am speaking here of seeking a wife who, under God, is seeking to walk as you walk and heading where you want to go. You should pray that the Lord would send you a woman with the generous heart of a true servant of God. She will be an invaluable blessing to you and to others.

But, most of all, simply be ready to serve. Take all the opportunities the Lord gives you to do good to others, and to bring glory to his name. Turn your nose up at nothing which helps you to develop the character of a true child of God. It may seem demeaning, but it is not beneath you. It may not feel very significant, but you do not know what it is worth. It may not be what you had in mind, but it might also be the very thing which the Lord uses to form Christ in you for enduring fruitfulness in the work of the kingdom. Nothing is more important than a Christlike disposition in fitting you to do the work which God has given you to do. It is in the path of cheerful duty that you are likely to enjoy the privileges and meet the opportunities which the Lord has appointed for you.

Eventual validations

God willing, if you give yourself to such a course, there

may come a time when a faithful church of Christ, the only body who can properly validate your sense of God's hand upon you, will be ready to put you to work. It may be on a limited scale; it may be with a view to something further. It may be that they will ultimately set you apart for vocational ministerial labour. You must wait for this. I know some churches move like treacle flowing uphill in winter; I know some people set a bar impossibly high. I hope that they will learn the lessons they should. But too many men are persuaded that they are the real deal when no faithful church has ever recognised in them the gifts and graces required of a true pastor of Christ's church.

I think of one young man who has already moved from one country to another in order to obtain rigorous training and healthy church oversight. Now he is wondering whether or not he has a long-term future where he is, or if it is God's will for him to return to his needy homeland to preach the gospel. What can I say to him? I can say, 'Go to your elders, those men who know you, love you and want to help you. Submit yourself to those whom the Lord has put over you, lay the matter before them and seek their counsel.' Another friend has agonised over whether or not he should leave his homeland and his present gospel opportunities in order better to equip himself, not least because the group with which he is associated is barely a church by any robust definition. For now, he stays, and so he looks for men who love the church to invest in him. In this way, he hopes that he can have some measure of more credible counsel and oversight as he pursues his studies. He trusts to have some confidence at the end that brothers who know what they are about can validate his sense of calling. Or think of the man we just mentioned who waited until he could find a healthy church to care for him rather than be thrust out by over-eager overseers who just wanted another notch on their belts. Despite long subsequent delays, he was eventually sent out into the harvest field, well-grounded and well-equipped for the hard labour that came his way.

It is in the church, the real church, the healthy church, the local church, that this work is primarily carried out. It is in the church that the weapons of this warfare are forged and fashioned. It is in the church that faithful men who have run the race pass the baton to those whom they have trained to run the next leg. It is in the church that proven and faithful men commit the truth of God to faithful men who will be able to teach others also. It is from the church that the next wave of faithful men, acclaimed by the church as Christ's men for Christ's time, are thrust out to serve the Lord of the harvest. By his grace, may there be a great in-gathering and up-growing in these needy days!

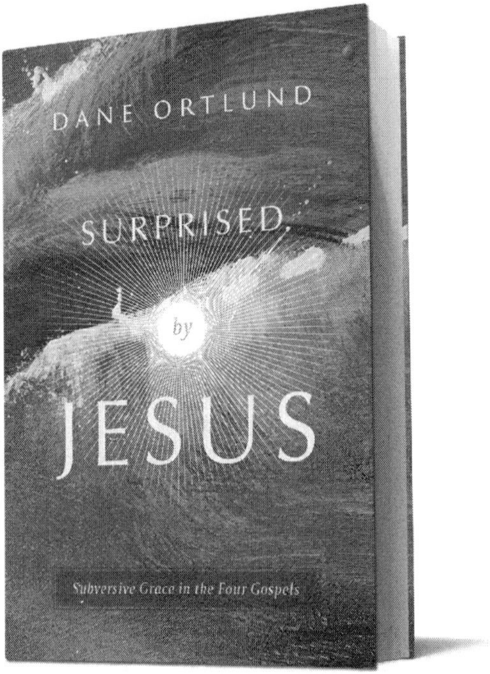
DANE ORTLUND
SURPRISED
by
JESUS
Subversive Grace in the Four Gospels